The Defining Moment

How Writers and Actors Build Characters

Christopher Riley and Kathy Riley

MICHAEL WIESE PRODUCTIONS

Published by Michael Wiese Productions
12400 Ventura Blvd. #1111
Studio City, CA 91604
(818) 379-8799, (818) 986-3408 (Fax)
mw@mwp.com
www.mwp.com
Manufactured in the
United States of America

This book was set in Garamond Premier Pro and Din Pro

Cover design by Johnny Ink
Interior design by Debbie Berne
Copyediting by Karen Krumpak

Library of Congress Cataloging-in-Publication Data
Names: Riley, Christopher, 1961– author. | Riley, Kathy, 1961– author.
Title: The defining moment : how writers and actors build characters / Christopher Riley and Kathy Riley.
Description: Studio City : Michael Wiese Productions, [2022]
Identifiers: LCCN 2021021204 | ISBN 9781615933372 (trade paperback)
Subjects: LCSH: Characters and characteristics in the performing arts. | Characters and characteristics in literature. | Acting. | Authorship.
Classification: LCC PN1590.C43 R55 2022 | DDC 792.02/8—dc23
LC record available at https://lccn.loc.gov/2021021204

PRAISE FOR *THE DEFINING MOMENT*

As animation directors, our stories are literally nothing without our characters. With *The Defining Moment*, Chris and Kathy have provided tools to help make your characters richer and fuller from the start! We've already begun utilizing some of the techniques that they've outlined. I challenge you to read this book and not do the same!
— Chris and Justin Copeland (DreamWorks Animation)

The key to great storytelling is memorable characters. Chris and Kathy Riley have written an essential and invaluable book to guide writers and actors on the crucial journey into the heart of dimensional, dynamic characters and to illuminate the best ways to bring them to life. I recommend this book to anyone involved in the creative process. It gets a place of honor on my bookshelf, next to Chris' *The Hollywood Standard.*
— Sheryl J. Anderson (creator and showrunner, *Sweet Magnolias*; writer-producer, *Ties That Bind*, *Charmed*)

In *The Defining Moment*, screenwriters Christopher and Kathy Riley generously reveal their own family's life-changing struggles to illustrate when a character is forced to transform. Covering well known character arcs (both fictional and historical), they delineate how a crucial moment, and choices thereafter, can enrich our storytelling and imbue the players with all-too-human complexity and pathos.
— Doreen Alexander Child (author of *Charlie Kaufman: Confessions of an Original Mind*)

If characters aren't emotionally authentic, there's simply no reason to keep watching a movie or reading a script (or to keep writing one, for that matter). Chris and Kathy dive deep into the exploration of what actors and screenwriters share in common — the creation of great characters — to provide insights that are enriching to storytellers of all types.
— Janet Scott Batchler (screenwriter, *Batman Forever*; screenwriting professor, USC School of Cinematic Arts)

Chris and Kathy Riley break open screenwriting with the kind of insight that reignites my own love of the craft, both as an actor and a writer. *The Defining Moment* takes the actor's instinct to find watershed moments and translates that approach for writers to find and create these crossroads on the page. It's an overdue look at how both disciplines (and more) come together to create the most compelling characters, which is what we all want to write. An inspiring read.
— Clare Sera (actor, *The Princess Diaries*; screenwriter, *Blended*, *Smallfoot*)

The Defining Moment is an important tool in the toolbox of any storyteller for bringing clarity, wisdom, and specificity to a process that can often feel amorphous. I cannot wait to see how this book encourages, inspires, and benefits artists.
— Joseph Barone (actor, *Homeland*, *American Horror Story*, *Justified*)

Chris and Kathy Riley have had a profound impact on my career as teachers, mentors, and (most importantly) friends. I'm thrilled that they're continuing to share their gifts and insights with the world through this fascinating new book. These are character-defining lessons for storytellers of all stripes.
— Scott Teems (screenwriter, *The Exorcist*, *Firestarter*, *Insidious: The Dark Realm*, *Halloween Kills*; writer-director, *Rectify*, *The Quarry*, *That Evening Sun*)

With keen insight and remarkable personal candor, Chris and Kathy Riley have written a book that had me looking back at everything I've ever written to see how it measures up . . . *The Defining Moment* will not only change the way you look at your characters; it may very well change the way you look at your life.
— Bill Marsilii (screenwriter, *Deja Vu*)

Novice screenwriters — and experienced ones, too — often struggle with character creation. The Rileys scrutinize pivotal scenes from films, television shows, and plays to show how dynamic events, choices, and actions define characters and increase the potential for audience involvement.
— Thomas Parham, PhD (writer, *JAG* and *Big Brother Jake*; Professor of Communication and Media Studies, Palm Beach Atlantic University)

Sometimes someone reminds you that circles are perfect and round, and you catch sight of the beauty and depth of what's always sat there in front of you. *The Defining Moment* is one of those books. It's not just for storytellers, it's for anyone wanting to understand why they are the way they are. As an actor, writer, and director, I only wish I would have had these insights thirty years ago, but I'm so very grateful to have them now.
— David Noroña (actor, *FBI: International, CSI: Vegas, Jack Ryan, The Mentalist, Weeds, One Tree Hill*)

Christopher and Kathy Riley have written the seminal book on character moments that embody memorable, personal moments in movies. From locating moments in characters and stories to recognizing how impactful these moments are, they've written an enriching, galvanizing book on character development that should be read by all storytellers. Wonderfully done.
— Dave Watson (editor, Movies Matter; author, *Walkabout Undone*)

To write a good script you have to understand what drives your character's behavior. In this book you will learn what questions to ask and how to truly investigate the backstory and motivations of them. "Defining moments" . . . we've all had them in real life, and so should your characters. By learning exactly what these moments are, your script will jump to life, and your audience will become completely invested in your story.
— Forris Day Jr. (Co-host, *Get Real: Indie Filmmakers* podcast)

The key to creating believable characters is discovering the moment that motivates every decision they make in a story. Christopher and Kathy Riley take writers and actors through a deep dive into the most defining moments of a character, as well as into exploring the moments that have most shaped you, to create better, more relatable characters.
— Tom Farr, writer and educator

I have always been a huge proponent of character being the foundation that all drama stems from. In *The Defining Moment*, Christopher and Kathy pull back the curtain to give us a deep, revealing look into the mythos of crafting characters from a viewpoint and breakdown I have yet to see explored. This is a great book to add to the library of any screenwriter, and one you can come back to again and again for inspiration. A true gem.
— Scott Parisien (award-winning screenwriter, *Foxter & Max*)

We've all been told to find the protagonist's flaw, but this is much too simplistic a way to define them. At the other end of the spectrum, we waste a significant amount of time creating character biographies with details that never end up in the story and, if they do, have no real weight. Defining moments are a significantly more efficient way to build characters, and focusing our energies into these key moments in the lives of our characters unlocks much more meaningful storytelling. With clear examples in films such as *Forrest Gump* and *Finding Nemo*, Christopher and Kathy Riley masterfully illustrate the power of using these key moments — not only in crafting characters, but in building the story itself. The Rileys also show how these moments help us to get in touch with the story of our own lives and communicate truthful experience on the page. Defining moments are evidenced by a before and after — for me, reading this book has created just such a before-and-after experience. I will never look at character creation the same way!
— Gray Jones (TV editor/writer; host of the *TV Writer Podcast*; partner of *Script Magazine*; author of *How to Break In To TV Writing: Insider Interviews*)

Christopher and Kathleen Riley have brought a fresh perspective to the storyteller's quest to realize tangible, compelling characters. Learning how these key moments build, develop, and ultimately complete or destroy the characters we create will make us more effective writers and actors. Highly recommended.
— Stuart Hazeldine (director, *The Shack*; writer-director, *Exam*; writer, *Agincourt*)

The Defining Moment is the rare "how to" book that also draws you in emotionally, offering powerful moments from film, TV, novels, plays, and the authors' lives that show how experiences become indelible and characters become memorable. For writers and actors, reading this book just might become the defining moment of your career.
— Dean Batali (showrunner, *That '70s Show* and *Good Witch*; writer-producer, *Buffy the Vampire Slayer*)

To our parents, Dale and Carol, Fred and Martha,
whose lives sparked ours
whose wounds shaped ours
whose strengths endure in ours

CONTENTS

FOREWORD

THIS BOOK IS ABOUT CHARACTER. There is a lot to unpack in that statement. Foremost, this book is about how to identify the key, defining moments in the lives of the characters we create for our stories, and how awareness of those critical events can help us write more compelling and realistic characters and more thrilling and emotionally charged scenes and situations.

At the same time, it's about character in a broader and deeper sense: character as the summing-up of a person's basic nature, habitual tendencies, and life choices. The building of character, through the adversities of life and a person's choices in reaction to those challenges, is one of the throughlines in this work. The authors make a valuable observation early on: the defining moments they speak of play the critical role in both the *formation* and the *transformation* of character. And that holds true on the page and in real life. Imagined characters in our stories and our own characters in daily life are formed and shaped by watershed moments deep in the past, but the process of forming and shaping continues throughout life, allowing for those transformative developments of character that are so exciting and satisfying for audiences, and are so impactful and memorable when they happen to us in reality.

Over the years, I have seen many books and concepts dealing with aspects of drama, storytelling, and the creation of characters. What strikes me is how compatible they all are. Rarely do they contradict one another. This book is one that fits into the matrix of current thinking, complementing and magnifying related systems such as the three-act structure, the hero's journey, and the "save the cat" model. The authors are walking down the same corridor of storytelling theory and practice that others have explored, but they have opened a door to a new room, dedicated to exploring one aspect — defining moments — in all possible depths. After visiting this room, you may find yourself rewalking the old familiar corridor with new eyes, noting how the defining moment idea is active and vital in all the story paradigms and character approaches. I went over all my ideas about structure and character, highlighting the defining moments — such as early loss or separation, meeting with a mentor, crossing a threshold, enduring a supreme ordeal, and resurrection — and I realized how the defining moments shaped characters, left them wounded, and sometimes lifted them to heights of self-realization.

Fittingly, the idea behind *The Defining Moment* came to these authors through a defining moment in their own lives, a fateful meeting with a fierce but benevolent mentor who demonstrated for them a method and a philosophy for creating believable, relatable characters. He taught them that characters are formed and, later, transformed by key moments; he showed them how to dig deep into character biographies to understand and accent those defining events. He gave them a valuable compass for both character and structure, because with knowledge of the defining moments, their stories could be built around revealing such formative events in the past and setting up transformative epiphanies in the character's future. We can be thankful that they took good care of this idea and nurtured it into a full-fledged body of knowledge. They also give us a vivid portrait of their mentor, who sounds like he must have been a real character in his own right.

From their rigorous training and their professional experiences of working with producers, writers, actors, and directors, they have distilled a systematic approach to this business of defining moments. They considered, categorized, and rationalized just about every imaginable variation of defining life moments: unforgettable episodes of loss; profound emotional changes; life-altering choices; emotional connections forged or broken; dreams shattered or awakened. In other words, the stuff of compelling drama. They present their findings with a clarity and order that I find admirable and that I believe will make the book extremely useful for writers and artists.

The subtitle of this work is "How Writers and Actors Build Characters," and the authors pay special attention to actors and their process of imagining the emotional life history of the people they play. They refer often to actors they have interviewed about how they create backstories for their characters, demonstrating the power of the defining moment idea, which should be part of the toolkit of every performer and artisan. In my brief time as an actor, I was not aware of the need to explore my character's defining moments, had no idea what shaped and motivated him, and therefore produced about as much dramatic intensity as the sofa. (Perhaps that's why a review stated "Mr. Vogler's acting defies publishable description.")

You'll find this book enjoyable to read because the authors are particularly skilled at the use of examples from movie scenes and structure, and they clearly like and appreciate the movies they talk about. A theory must be backed up and illustrated by examples, and having been challenged to come up with representative movie scenes and characters to support my ideas, I am impressed by their dexterity with this part of the assignment. It requires careful watching and rewatching of films so that you fully understand the intentions of each scene, its context within the overall plot, and even its relationship to similar scenes in other movies. You have to be incredibly precise about describing the movie because film fanatics will pounce on you for the slightest inaccuracy. I get the feeling the authors spent many hours viewing films, extracting essential scenes to support their points, discussing them, and then describing them succinctly without getting bogged in details. Masterfully, they present convincing cinematic evidence for their approach and will lead you either to explore some movies you might have missed or to revisit scenes in beloved classics, appreciating them with fresh eyes through the lens of the defining moment concept.

The authors assert that to understand your characters, you must understand yourself. I think they're right. In dealing with writers as an executive and story consultant, and in writing stories myself, I have learned that we sometimes cannot transcend the boundaries of our own personalities and experiences. It's hard for someone who has not suffered and lost, who has not tried and failed, to write believably about characters who suffer, lose, try, and fail. I think the reason most of us write stories in the first place is to know ourselves better. Each new assignment is a test of character: Will I have the nerve and endurance to finish this work? Do I have deep enough understanding of my characters and their emotional life history? Can I find parallels in my own emotional life that give me insight into what my characters have survived and are about to face?

The Rileys recommend exploring the defining moments in your own life, and they give some useful guidelines for this practice. I found myself examining my own twisting path through life and discovered that, yes, there had been many of these defining "before and after" moments when I made critical choices and experienced changes of fortune, moments of loss and wounding, instants when dreams died or were born. It even made me wonder what epiphanies and transformative moments are waiting for me on life's highway. In these pages, I suspect you will follow a similar path, expanding your ideas about character and structure and empowering yourself to write more emotionally moving stories and authentic characters, but also glancing in the mirror now and then to reflect on the defining before-and-after moments of your life and the revelations, reconciliations, and breakthroughs yet to come.

Christopher Vogler
Author of *The Writer's Journey: Mythic Structure for Writers*

INTRODUCTION

Building Deep Characters

WHO ARE WE, WE WRITERS AND ACTORS?

Along with directors, editors, and every kind of storyteller, we share one astonishing trait. We bring characters into the world.

We make women. And men. And children. We make robots and monsters and hobbits. Mobsters and clown fish. Singing teapots and chimney sweeps. Presidents and assassins. Living and breathing, our offspring live lives separate from our own, surprising us, defying us, speaking lines we don't premeditate, making choices that dismay, delight, and shock us.

We make them grow and suffer, fight and fall in love. When we're at our best, we deliver into the world full-bodied persons — sometimes clad in fish flesh or exotic alien tissues, other times wrapped in frames as ordinary and human as dust. Once delivered, our offspring cavort, quest, strive, make love, transform, suffer, heal, kill, and die upon the screen, the stage, and the page.

Darth Vader. Scarlett O'Hara. Anton Chigurh. Ophelia. Forrest Gump. Virgil Tibbs. Dr. Welby. Marianne Dashwood. T'Challa. Lady Macbeth. Vito Corleone. Batman. Frodo. Hamlet. Jack Sparrow. Hedda Gabler. Mickey Mouse. Michael Scott. Nemo. Juno. Jojo Rabbit. Indiana Jones. Frasier Crane. Mary

Poppins. Aslan. Hannibal Lecter. Clarice Starling. Walter White. Malcolm X. Alexander Hamilton. Rocky Balboa. Pinocchio.

Each of these indelible characters, more human than humans, more memorable than too many of the actual people we've known, have emerged from the wombs of our imaginations and toil. They have emerged filled with purpose and pain, blood and sinew — or circuit boards and gears. They've emerged after we've worked alone in protracted isolation until they've spilled onto the pages of a novel. Or they've emerged after we've worked in fierce collaboration on a stage, in a writers' room, or on a film set.

Once delivered, these characters do what all living things do: They grow. They change. They transform. Lajos Egri writes in his classic treatise on character, *The Art of Dramatic Writing*, "Life is change . . . Every human being is in a state of constant fluctuation and change. Nothing is static in nature, least of all man."

For those of us who write, direct, and play these characters into existence, we need a way to understand two related processes. First, by what means are characters formed before they arrive at what Egri calls the "point of attack" — that is, the moment when the curtain goes up and the telling of the story begins? And second, once the telling has begun, by what means do characters grow bigger or smaller, wiser or more foolish, braver or more cowardly, more or less able, or ruthless, or beautiful, as we watch? How we conceive, gestate, and birth lifelike characters and how we raise them to maturity is the subject of this book.

Consider the opening scene from the 2003 Pixar film *Finding Nemo*.

Two clown fish in love, Marlin and Coral, have just moved into their new ocean home on the seafloor near the drop-off from the shallows into the deep. Coral has laid hundreds of eggs in a cave beneath their home. The happy couple await the hatching of their many offspring, carefree, brimming with dreams of a future populated by hundreds of little Marlin Juniors and Coral Juniors and perhaps one son named Nemo.

And then the dream turns to nightmare. A barracuda attacks. As Marlin fights to defend his family, he begs Coral to take shelter inside their home. But Marlin is no match for the barracuda, and Coral can't bear to retreat and leave her eggs unprotected. As Coral darts toward the opening to the cave that holds her eggs, the barracuda bludgeons Marlin unconscious. The screen goes dark.

When Marlin awakes, the barracuda is gone. So is Coral. The heartbroken husband can hardly bear to look inside the cave. When he does, he discovers that the eggs, like Coral, are no more. They've been cleaned out, annihilated. All but one solitary orange egg with an eye flickering within, all that remains of Marlin's family, his love, his dreams.

In that moment of unimaginable grief, Marlin names his unhatched baby Nemo. And he makes a pledge. "I'll never let anything happen to you, Nemo."

This is the audacious opening scene of a children's movie. What does it contribute to *Finding Nemo*? For starters, it's riveting storytelling. It's a great scene to watch for the length of time we're watching it. But its value to the movie lasts far longer than the running time of the scene itself. The scene dredges out emotional depths, creating a sense of loss that invests the entire rest of the film with a gravitas it would otherwise lack. Experiencing that moment of tragedy with Marlin informs our understanding of the bereaved father's overprotective parenting and heightens our sense of stakes when Nemo, Marlin's only surviving family, is captured and imperiled. That opening scene makes a profound contribution to the way the audience *feels* the entire rest of the story. And it does more.

It transforms Marlin. The adventure-loving fish who began the story having chosen a home where his growing family would live literally *on the edge* becomes an anxious father, hovering and hypervigilant, driven no longer by a hunger for adventure but by a compulsion to protect. If we didn't witness his moment of catastrophic damage, Marlin's neurosis would seem to us a character quirk and little more. We wouldn't feel the tragic weight of the defining moment of which his neurosis is an echo.

Finding Nemo's opening scene makes a further essential contribution to the story. It creates the need for Marlin's *future transformation*. The bereaved, overprotective father needs to grow. His first defining moment creates the need for a second. The first wounded him. The second, which may or may not come, must heal him — for Marlin's sake, and for the sake of his son.

If we met Marlin at some point after the events depicted in the opening scene of *Finding Nemo*, we wouldn't be able to understand him. We certainly couldn't say in any true sense that we knew him, if we knew nothing of that moment. And, worse, we wouldn't care.

And the storyteller's job is to make the audience care.

Consider next the restaurant scene from the 1972 gangster film *The Godfather*.

It's the winter of 1945 in New York City. Michael Corleone is a war hero, just home from Europe, where he fought as a Marine. Michael leads a life in sharp contrast to that of his father, Vito Corleone, head of a notorious crime family. Michael rejoins his family at a time of dangerous instability. A new boss, Sollozzo, is muscling in on Corleone turf. When Vito, the Godfather, refuses to yield to Sollozzo's advances, Sollozzo has Vito gunned down. Five bullets go into the Godfather's back. And though Don Corleone survives the immediate attack, his life remains under threat from his enemies. Michael, whom the screenplay by Mario Puzo and Francis Ford Coppola calls a "high-class college kid" who "never wanted to get mixed up in the family business," now feels the urgent need to step forward and defend his father. He becomes convinced that both the interloper Sollozzo and McCluskey, the corrupt police captain who serves as Sollozzo's bodyguard, must be killed.

Tom Hagen, the family's consiglieri, warns, "What you have to understand is that while Sollozzo is guarded like this, he's invulnerable. Nobody has ever gunned down a New York police captain. Never. It would be disastrous."

Michael insists, "We can't wait. No matter what Sollozzo says about a deal, he's figuring out how to kill Pop. You have to get Sollozzo now."

And then Michael suggests a plan that astonishes Hagen and the rest of the family. Michael will meet with Sollozzo and McCluskey and kill them both. The high-class college kid, the war hero who never wanted to get mixed up in the family business, will commit the murders himself.

In the screenplay, Michael contrives to have a gun planted at the Luna Azure, the restaurant where the meeting will take place. He sits across the table from his enemies and breaks bread with them. Then he excuses himself to the bathroom and retrieves the hidden gun.

"He takes a deep breath," the script reads, "and shoves it under his waistband." And then the script adds a curious notation. "For some unexplainable reason he hesitates once again, deliberately washes his hands and dries them. Then he goes out."

The story seems to pause at this moment, to take a breath, anticipating the plunge. A moment of action approaches, the storytellers understand, that will transform Michael in a way that will shape the rest of the movie and, it turns out, its sequels.

After this pause, Michael returns to take his seat at the table.

The screenplay tells us, "Sollozzo begins to speak in Sicilian once again but Michael's heart is pounding so hard he can barely hear him." More anticipation of what's to come, more underscoring of the importance of what's about to transpire. And then it happens. Without warning, the script tells us, Michael shoves the table away from him and shoots Sollozzo and then McCluskey.

> Michael is wildly at a peak. He starts to move out. His hand: is frozen by his side, still gripping the gun.
>
> He moves, not letting the gun go.
>
> Michael's face; frozen in its expression.
>
> His hand: still holding the gun.
>
> His face: finally he closes his eyes.
>
> His hand relaxes, the gun falls to the floor with a dull thud. He walks quickly out of the restaurant, looks back.
>
> He sees a frozen tableau of the murder; as though it had been recreated in wax.
>
> Then he leaves.

The moment is elongated, emphasized, spotlit. Why? Because this is the moment that makes Michael Corleone what he will become, the successor to his father, the next Godfather. In this moment, Michael is redefined, remade, reborn. He embraces a ruthlessness that will define him and dictate his future.

If we met Michael Corleone at some point after this event, we wouldn't be able to understand him, and we certainly couldn't say in any true sense that we knew him if we knew nothing of this moment.

What does this moment contribute to *The Godfather*? As with the opening scene of *Finding Nemo*, it's riveting storytelling. Every second we're with Michael at the Luna Azure, our eyes remain glued to the screen. But its value to the movie lasts far longer than the scene itself. The scene crowns Michael as the protagonist of the film, the prime mover, his father's successor. It informs our understanding of every action Michael takes thereafter. Because we understand the love of family that moved Michael to kill, because we were with him when he conceived, planned, and carried out the twin murders, we understand and relate to and continue to root for Michael in ways we otherwise never could. And the moment does more.

It transforms Michael. The clean-cut, law-abiding Marine who wanted to have nothing to do with his family's criminal enterprise — whose own crime boss father wanted him to have nothing to do with that business — becomes a bold and ruthless cop killer, a man who has now done what had never been done before, a man who might now do anything. If we didn't witness his moment of dramatic moral change, Michael's ruthlessness would seem a convenient character trait for a gangster movie but little more. We wouldn't comprehend its profoundly human roots or remain emotionally invested in his character as the fullness of his resulting family tragedy unfolds.

The restaurant scene in *The Godfather* makes a further essential contribution to the story. It creates the need for Michael to be saved and sets up much of what follows. It creates the necessity for Michael to flee to Italy so that his life can be saved. And it sets up our desire for Michael to return to Kay so that his soul can be saved. This ruthless, morally damaged man needs to grow. That he doesn't grow in the ways for which we intuitively yearn — that no second defining moment of redemption ever takes place — fuels the manifold tragedy of the story for Fredo, for Kay, for their unborn son, and for Michael himself.

These two scenes, these two moments — one from an animated family film and one from a gangster drama for adults — have an outsized emotional impact on the audience, along with an enduring power to shape and define the characters at their core. They reveal that our best stories explore more than characters. They explore character *formation* and *transformation*. Sometimes the shaping of characters takes place in slow, smooth, steadily bending arcs, but other times in sudden, jagged, cataclysmic moments.

The coming chapters will explore the remarkable power of a small number of discrete moments to effect dramatic and lasting character change. These moments rip characters open, exposing them naked to the gaze of the audience, infusing them with depth, psychological authenticity, and emotional resonance, shaping characters who linger in our memories and demand we care.

Spoiler alert: Throughout this book, we will describe pivotal moments from film, television, books, and the stage. We must describe these moments to illustrate the contribution such moments make to the art of character creation, development, and revelation. When we reference the title of a work you haven't watched or read, you have three options. First, you can plunge ahead reading our description, and what's spoiled is spoiled. Second, you can skip that part of the book and keep yourself unspoiled. Third, you can put down this book and immediately race off to watch or read the wonderful work we're about to describe, then return with fresh knowledge and appreciation of that work.

* * *

One further introduction:

As stories have storytellers, books have authors. This one has Christopher and Kathy Riley, two lifelong storytellers and, increasingly, these days, story listeners. We moved to Hollywood decades ago, freshly married, freshly college-minted, towing a U-Haul trailer packed with our wedding presents still in their boxes, and with no earthly idea how to tell stories that deserved the attention of millions of people. In the years since, we've become screenwriters and authors and teachers of the best of what we've learned along the way. This book delves into what we've come to understand about creating emotionally authentic characters who grow as they struggle. It does so from the point of view of a pair of screenwriters. We don't act. We're not authorities on acting. But we believe that writers and actors have much to teach one another about how we understand the work all of us do with characters. As our friend Joseph Barone, a Los Angeles–based actor, told us, "In the entertainment profession, we are all storytellers. We're coming at it from different angles, but ultimately we're all trying to tell the story."

Tony Hale, the celebrated comic actor who earned a raft of Emmy and Screen Actors Guild awards and nominations playing Buster Bluth in the television series *Arrested Development* and Gary Walsh in the HBO series *Veep*, described to us an experience he had on a recent project. "It was a really interesting script," remembered Hale. But during production, Hale encountered something in the script that gave him pause. "There was a jarring moment that needed to be massaged." He told the writer/director, "I just don't think I would do this." His colleague's response, recalled Hale, demonstrated that he cared more about the story itself than he did about asserting his ownership of the words on the page. "He cared about the piece, he cared about the message," said Hale. The filmmaker welcomed the veteran actor's insights and incorporated them into the film. Hale explained, "If you can place your ego to the side and allow others to speak into the process, and if you can trust the actor you've hired, really trusting his or her gut, really separate your ego, it can make it make sense." Of course, important insights flow in the other direction, too, from writers and directors to actors. "Actors are desperate for help arranging what's in the writer or director's mind. To get that feedback is gold," said Hale. We hope this book furthers a conversation between our disciplines that will enrich all of us with the many lessons we can teach one another.

As we explore the ways writers, directors, and actors create characters of depth and complexity, we will make the claim that to understand the characters to whom you give birth, you must understand yourself. This suggests that we the authors have needed to come to some understanding of ourselves. In the pages that follow, when we urge you to search for the moments that define you, we will offer, by way of example, such moments of our own. These moments are personal. Some are painful. They include moments of injury and moments of healing. Telling them makes us vulnerable. They will reveal us. But we trust they will help you recognize the pivotal moments in your own history. And we hope they will encourage and equip you to reveal yourself, both in the characters you create and in the life you lead. We begin as strangers to one another. Through the stories all of us will tell in the years to come and the many characters we each have yet to create, we hope that, somehow, we'll come to know one another.

1.
The Essential Insight of Defining Moments

"I don't need to know if there's gum on your shoe,
I just need to know how you got that scar."

AS STORYTELLERS, WE LONG TO DO JUSTICE TO OUR CHARACTERS. WE yearn to present more than two-dimensional caricatures. We hope to offer the audience deep, complicated, recognizable, flawed people like us. But whenever we approach this work, we stand humbled before its demands.

Persons — and, by extension, characters — are *infinitely* complex. They defy any effort to make a full inventory of their minds, their personalities, their purses, their pasts or their souls. They exceed our capacity to comprehend. Even when we live inside our own bodies and enjoy direct access to our own thoughts, to our singular, invisible inner life, the possibility continues that decade after decade we make new discoveries about and gain deeper insights into ourselves. How then can we hope to gain omniscience about another person or character? We can't.

What can we do then, we who labor to give birth to lifelike characters who bear the wounds of fulsome pasts and who struggle and transform before the captivated eyes of an audience that laughs and sighs and thinks, "Yes, that's how it is for me, too"? What can we know about our characters? Or, more to the point, what *must* we know?

The Moment We Discovered Defining Moments

During the early years of our development as screenwriters, we wrote a screenplay for a courtroom thriller we titled *In Defense of Josef Mengele*. It was a what-if. "What if the notorious Angel of Death of Auschwitz returned to modern day Germany to stand trial? And what if he was represented at trial by an idealistic attorney committed to telling the truth about Mengele's monstrous actions during the war? What could we learn about a doctor who became a monster? And what could we learn about ourselves?"

We managed to get the script into the hands of a gruff, gifted television writer-producer named Coleman Luck. At the time we met him, he was writing and producing on the hour-long television series *The Equalizer*. He phoned us and complimented our script and told us he didn't think we were looking at an immediate sale, but offered to mentor us as we rewrote. Luck saw life as alive with meaning and was committed to telling stories that added up to something. He had been a combat infantry officer in Vietnam and become a man who didn't mince words. We sat with him in his office at Universal, where he displayed a broadsword on top of his coffee table, and he predicted that if we chose to work with him, he would push us so hard toward excellence that we would come to hate him. We thought he was joking. He wasn't. And though we never did grow to hate him, he did push us to work harder than we had imagined any writer worked, digging into our characters, asking ever more penetrating questions about them, excavating the truth about who they were, what had made them thus, and by what means they might change under the pressures the story could bring to bear.

One day, as we wrestled with our understanding of our characters, Luck explained his theory of what he called *defining moments*. Each of us, he believed, is the product of a handful of pivotal experiences or decisions, perhaps as few as five or six in a lifetime, that have shaped our course and made us who we've become. These experiences and decisions create moments of *before* and *after*. We can speak of the time before the divorce and the time after. The time before and after the fire or the diagnosis, or the time before and after two lovers met. If you are our friend, you may come to know some of our defining moments, the moments that have scarred us, given birth to our dreams, even healed us. The more of these moments you know, the better you may be said to know us. And so it was, Luck proposed, with our characters. Discovering that handful of moments that have defined a character could become the key to understanding the deepest and most important truths of that character.

He gave us the homework of searching for the five or six moments that had defined each of the main characters in our screenplay. Once we'd found those moments, Luck told us, we should describe each one in a paragraph, like a short dramatic scene. We spent the next week or so interrogating our characters — Mengele, his attorney Peter Rohm, Peter's grandmother Hilde — exploring their childhoods, their youths, the years leading up to the opening of our movie, the key experiences and decisions that had formed the people we met at fade in. But we didn't stop with an examination of our characters' pasts. We searched the pages of our own script for clues about how the events and choices that took place after the movie began reshaped and redefined our characters. We sought to understand or sharpen the pivotal moments that made up, like links in a chain, the arcs of our characters as they grew and changed. We even allowed ourselves to imagine moments that might take place after the final fade-out, moments that the trajectory of our story's character transformations suggested might lie ahead.

We returned to Luck's office with our handful of stories for each of our main characters and with a degree of insight into those characters that had dramatically deepened. We had a clearer sense of what they might say and do under pressure. Our connection to them felt more intimate. We derived new scenes for our script that provided the actors who would eventually play the roles deeper insight into their characters. Those scenes created the opportunity for the actors and director to reveal those characters onscreen to an audience that could form intimate connections with those characters. They made it possible for the audience to care.

The script got better.

Eventually retitled *After the Truth*, this script launched our careers as writers, earned us representation at one of Hollywood's top talent agencies, and sold to German producer Werner Koenig. The film was directed by the talented Roland Suso Richter and starred the extraordinary Götz George as Mengele and Kai Wiesinger as Rohm. While the film won multiple international awards, it seems significant in this context that the most prestigious award for which the film was nominated, the European Film Award, was an *acting* award for George's masterfully human and disturbing portrayal of Mengele. And this seems to us evidence that Luck's insight into character had paid off in a successful collaboration between writers, director, actors, and, our most important collaborators, the members of the audience.

Defining Moments Make Deep Character Development Possible

If Luck was right, and we're convinced he was, we don't need to know every one of the infinite number of details about a character. For writers, directors, and actors, this is good news. Knowing our characters becomes possible.

Imagine, for example, that we're telling the story of an overprotective clown fish named Marlin, a father who perseverates over the safety of his son, Nemo. Over the course of the story, we plan for Marlin's hypervigilant parenting to drive a wedge between him and his son. And then that son, despite Marlin's restrictive supervision, strays into dangerous waters, is captured and carried into captivity far from home. We envision a journey of growth during which Marlin will need to confront and overcome his limitations in order to rescue and reconcile with Nemo. Following Luck's thinking, we might look at this character dynamic and subsequent arc and ask, "How did Marlin become so overprotective? What fear drives him? What loss has he suffered that has given birth to such a fear?" And this line of inquiry might lead us to discover the moment of tragic loss* that opens *Finding Nemo*, shapes Marlin, invests us deeply in Marlin's cause, provides the starting point for his inner journey, and deepens our emotional connection to the entire film. And all of this becomes possible not because we know what Marlin ate for breakfast but because we located the moment that defined him.

This insight, once gained, may seem obvious. We do believe it is simple and quickly grasped. But like many powerful truths, the idea gains utility and provides benefit to writers, directors, and

---

* For a more complete description of this moment, see the Introduction.

actors only when we apply it in our actual lives and work. Luck spoke to us about defining moments for only a few minutes. We've spent the decades since that conversation plumbing the depths of this idea and endeavoring to harness its power in the stories we tell.

Why We Resist This Insight

This imperative to plumb our characters' depths runs hard against our culture and instincts. People we meet ask us what we do, what we're working on, who we know, what we drive, where we live. Few ask, "What is the moment that dealt you your most crippling blow?" or "At what instant was your dream for your work or your family life born?" or "How have you experienced healing from your most grievous wound?" Questions like that can clear a room. For many of us, our instinct is to hide. The pressure of our culture, of our upbringing in polite society, of the norms of interaction meant to insulate us from awkward social interactions, demands that we lie to one another. The truth is, in our real lives we too rarely invite or offer honesty and intimacy. When we're face to face, we prefer to talk about our successes, not our defeats; our credits, not our crises; our Teslas, not our tragedies. But in our giving and receiving of stories on the screen, on the stage and on the page, the longing to know and be known finds an arena in which it can thrive. Storytelling allows us to gaze on the inner life, struggles, and wounds of another. Films, television, books, and plays invite us to see one another as we are. We can look without looking away. We can bear to see. And when we act in the role of the storyteller, our souls can dare to disrobe and bear to be seen. We believe this seeing and being seen represents one of the most primal and powerful attractions of storytelling for audience and storyteller alike.

And what exactly do we long to see and know? When we think about the intimate encounters we've experienced with characters in our favorite films, television, plays, and books, we don't think primarily about what Robert McKee in his landmark book *Story** calls *characterization*: "the sum of all observable qualities of a human being, everything knowable through careful scrutiny... all aspects of humanity we could know by taking notes on someone day in and day out." Those things are interesting and often amusing. But when we think about the characters with whom we've experienced our strongest and most intimate encounters, we think about what McKee calls *true character*, which he says "is revealed in the choices a human being makes under pressure — the greater the pressure, the deeper the revelation, the truer the choice to the character's essential nature." It isn't Forrest Gump's leg braces that attach us to him throughout his many improbable adventures, from the jungles of Vietnam to the waters of the Gulf to the White House; it's his pure and relentless love of Jenny, a love born in a defining moment when Forrest meets his golden-haired girl on the school bus and is forever changed.

There's another reason we resist the work required to plumb our characters' depths. We get ahead of ourselves. We get excited about what our characters are about to say and do. Often a story's surface action, to borrow a term from author Claudia Hunter Johnson, sparkles so brightly that we're tempted to race ahead, following our characters as they pursue some high-stakes goal through impossible obstacles. With our hearts pounding and legs churning, we race from one character action to the next, from one struggle to another, focused solely on *what* our characters do because it's so blasted interesting or amusing or audacious, but neglecting to ask *why* they do what they do.

Many times in the course of developing stories, we've been tempted to shortcut the process. We know enough, we think. Our heroine needs to get her dying child to a doctor on the other side

---

* Robert McKee, *Story: Substance, Structure, Style, and the Principles of Screenwriting*, HarperEntertainment, 1977.

of the front lines, deep in enemy territory. Her motivation is primal, and the clock is ticking. We can imagine the risks she'll take, how she'll negotiate the betrayal of allies and the unexpected assistance of enemies. We envision the moment she reaches the hospital where the doctor works and how it will feel when he recognizes her as an enemy and nonetheless saves her child — or refuses in that final desperate moment to provide treatment. What more do we need to know? And so we rush ahead, writing or directing or acting those intensely dramatic scenes, but operating at a superficial level that prevents us from knowing or making known a character at the greatest possible depth.

The creation of character-defining moments requires discipline and a kind of love for our characters. It demands that we resist the temptation to race ahead. It requires us to slow down and think about our characters, listen to them, study them. "What happened to you," we must ask with patience and compassion, "to make you this way?" We understand this mother has a dying child, but only she can tell us what being a mother means to *her* and how she, unique among all women, came to motherhood. How did that moment when her newborn was first placed in her arms change her? From what to what was she changed? Only when we take the time and invest the effort, only when we give them our precious attention, will our characters share these intimate secrets with us.

What Does All This Hard Work Get Us?

Let's say we take the time to unearth our characters' defining moments. What benefits accrue from knowledge of these events?

We propose that defining moments can provide the key to:

- understanding the invisible forces that drive and impede our characters

- commanding the attention of our audience
- deepening the audience's emotional investment in our characters
- tracking and dramatizing character growth and transformation
- energizing the performance of actors who've come into contact with the deepest forces driving their characters
- equipping writers, directors, actors, and all of our creative collaborators as we work together telling deep, honest, and moving stories

We'll examine those benefits one at a time.

Understanding the Invisible Forces That Drive and Impede Our Characters

Forrest Gump inspires a young Elvis Presley's distinctive dance style. He plays college football. He rescues wounded soldiers in Vietnam. He plays ping-pong in China. He visits the White House. He speaks at a war protest on the National Mall. He founds a shrimping business. He invests in Apple. He donates to the International Church of the Foursquare Gospel. He mows lawns. He runs countless miles. He does a head-spinning variety of things, and yet his story holds together as if all of these disconnected actions are one. What holds this nutty tale together?

We can talk about Forrest Gump's low IQ. His distinctive manner of speaking. His odd posture. His innocence. All those details matter. None explains why he does what he does. None reveals the glue that holds his story together. It isn't his IQ or his posture or his innocence. What is it?

It's his love for Jenny.

That love drives him to write her letters every day he's in Vietnam and to follow her advice when danger comes. His love for Jenny drives him to name a fleet of shrimping boats after her and to crash a Black Panther party and to wade into the Reflecting Pool and to welcome her into his home and care for her through her final illness and cherish her memory and raise her son. Forrest Gump's love for Jenny drives his actions and unifies the movie. That love defines him.

Is there a single, critical moment when this relationship is born? In fact, there is. In the screenplay by Eric Roth, based on the novel by Winston Groom, Forrest himself describes that moment, beginning as his younger self boards the school bus on his first day of school. None of the kids will let him sit beside them. And as young Forrest stands in the aisle looking for a seat, adult Forrest narrates, "You know, it's funny what a young man recollects. 'Cause I don't remember being born." And, as if to drive home the point that this moment stands unique in his memory, he continues, "I don't recall what I got for my first Christmas and I don't know when I went on my first outdoor picnic. But I do remember the first time I heard the sweetest voice in the wide world."

"You can sit here if you want," says Jenny Curran, a golden-haired girl about Forrest's age.

Adult Forrest says, "I had never seen anything so beautiful in my life. She was like an angel."

Forrest takes the seat next to Jenny, they introduce themselves to one another, and their friendship is born.

"From that day on," recalls Forrest, "we was always together. Jenny and me was like peas and carrots. She was my most special friend. My only friend."

Notice the before-and-after language Forrest uses: "From that day on." Before that moment, he had no friend. After that moment, he had Jenny. And his love for Jenny defines him and drives his actions to the day of her death and beyond. If we're ignorant of the difference meeting Jenny makes in Forrest's life, we don't know Forrest Gump. Knowing about their meeting and its significance provides the key to comprehending the powerful and invisible forces that drive this iconic movie character.

We've already discussed the tragic opening scene of *Finding Nemo* and its enduring impact on Marlin. The damage inflicted on his psyche by that moment of loss affects him in many ways. It puts an end to his spirit of adventure. It transforms him into a fearful, overly restrictive parent. It creates a barrier between him and his only surviving child. If we're ignorant of Marlin's defining moment, we don't know Marlin. Knowing about that moment provides the key to comprehending the powerful and invisible forces that impede this beloved movie character.

Commanding the Attention of Our Audience

Alfred Hitchcock famously said, "Drama is life with the dull bits cut out." He's right, of course. We don't want to watch the bits where nothing happens. Nor do we want to watch the long, slow bits where something might be happening but happens so slowly that it's imperceptible. That's why in the history of cinema, we don't have any great paint-drying scenes. It's why Shakespeare and Ibsen failed to provide any memorable grass-growing or glacier-creeping scenes. We have no interest in watching the earth's tectonic plates creep, century by century, millimeter by millimeter, or the ultra slow-motion ooze of magma miles beneath our wheat fields. As a great white shark hunts for prey, our eye scans for change. When nothing changes, our attention wanders. But when a volcano rumbles and the magma explodes into the sky, leveling forests and gushing rivers of molten rock, we take notice. The slow creep of the glacier bores us; the calving of massive icebergs that plunge into the sea and create tsunamis as tall as skyscrapers fascinates. Nine months of gestation doesn't make for spellbinding observation; the moment of birth does.

We were living in Los Angeles on the morning of January 17, Martin Luther King Jr. Day, 1994. At the time, we lived only a few miles from Northridge, the spot in the San Fernando Valley where, at 4:30 a.m., a blind thrust fault ruptured. Megatons of energy were released. Violent shock waves radiated through the city. Freeway overpasses collapsed. Apartment buildings crumbled. Shopping malls caved in. Parking structures pancaked. We awoke to our world writhing in darkness, our bed bucking as if an enraged giant lay beneath, intent on shaking the life out of us. Our young children were screaming in their beds, but we couldn't hear them over the screaming of the house itself. For the first time since moving to California and experiencing several less intense seismic events, we understood how people die in earthquakes.

The initial shock lasted between ten and twenty seconds. The speed at which the ground moved was the highest ever recorded. Our home and our family survived. Many others didn't. Fifty-seven of our fellow Angelenos died that morning. Almost nine thousand were hurt. Property damage was counted in the tens of billions of dollars. The mountain outside the window of the house where we live today grew three feet taller. All in between ten and twenty seconds. It was a moment that captured our attention. While it lasted, we couldn't think of anything else. It was as intensely dramatic as any moment we've experienced in our lives.

This is the power of defining moments to command our attention and our care.

We pay attention to the moments of change. And defining moments are the moments of eruption, of seismic shaking, of birth and death. They are the moments of greatest change. Discovering them and employing them in our storytelling provides a key to capturing the attention and care of an audience.

Deepening the Audience's Emotional Investment in Our Characters

When we moved to Los Angeles, we brought a script Chris had written in college. During our first months in town, we happened to meet a producer who became a friend, and he offered to read that script. It was the first time an industry professional was laying eyes on work either of us had done, and we looked forward to enthusiastic feedback and some sort of open door to move forward in our careers as baby screenwriters.

Instead, what we heard the next time we saw the producer was this: "I read your script. If I didn't like you, I wouldn't have read past the first ten pages."

Chris stammered something like, "Oh." And then, "Why?"

The producer responded with blunt words. "I didn't care about your characters."

Those words did more than sting. They made Chris question whether he even belonged in Hollywood. He suddenly doubted whether he had what it took to become a professional screenwriter if he couldn't accomplish that most fundamental storytelling task: making a reader give a rip about his characters.

After spending twenty-four miserable hours contemplating a retreat home to Kansas, Chris picked himself off the floor, and together we asked ourselves a question we would need to answer if we were going to progress as storytellers: "How do we make people care about our characters?"

Defining moments—while not the complete answer—provide an important key to unlocking the answer to that question.

When we see Marlin suffer the loss of his family, we gain more than an understanding of the forces that drive and impede him. Our hearts are moved. We gain a deep sense of investment in his well-being. We feel an emotional stake in his story. We attach to him. We begin to care what happens to Marlin. And when Nemo is taken captive, we root intensely for Marlin to rescue his only surviving child. If we're an actor, director, or producer reading the script, we keep turning the pages.

Tracking and Dramatizing Character Growth and Transformation

In the exquisite 2015 film *Room*, written by Emma Donoghue and directed by Lenny Abrahamson, actress Brie Larson plays Joy Newsome, a young woman who was abducted as a teenager and has been held captive ever since in her abductor's backyard shed. When the film begins, Joy has spent seven years imprisoned this way, has given birth to a son she calls Jack (played by Jason Tremblay), has raised him in this confined world she and her son call "Room," and is preparing to celebrate Jack's fifth birthday. Jack is Joy's entire world, and Joy has employed her immense love and creativity to transform their prison cell into an entire world for Jack. Against all odds, she has protected him from the psychological damage that should have been unavoidable, growing up where he has. But when Joy's captor, a barely seen figure she calls Old Nick, takes ominous notice of Jack, Joy hatches an ingenious plan to help Jack escape. At incalculable emotional cost to herself, Joy launches Jack out of Room and into the wide world he's never known. The escape attempt itself unfolds in a sequence so harrowing, so uncertain, so freighted with physical and emotional stakes it's almost unwatchable. The escape attempt succeeds. Jack makes it to safety. He assists the police in finding and freeing his mother. And that's just the story up to the movie's midpoint. Because while mother and son have completed their physical escape, they have yet to make their emotional escape. Joy's mother, played by Joan Allen, embraces her daughter and grandson with a full heart.

Joy's father, played by William H. Macy, can't. When he looks at Joy, all he can see is the pain of having lost her for all those years. And when he looks at Jack, all he can see is the kidnapper who raped his daughter and fathered this child. Unable to bear Jack's presence, Macy's character departs, leaving his daughter to negotiate the rest of her perilous journey without his support.

Without describing the remainder of the story, which depicts additional character growth, we can point to multiple defining moments implicit in the lives of these characters that allow us to track their transformation.

To begin, we can point to the moment of Joy's abduction. For Joy, her mother, and her father, this event creates a moment of before and after. It's a moment that redirects each of their lives in dramatic ways. For Joy, the changes are obvious. Instead of leading the life of a typical high school student, she becomes a prisoner and sex slave. For her parents, their lives become consumed with the search for their daughter and the ongoing grief of her loss.

For Joy, the birth of Jack represents a further defining moment. Before his birth, she dwelt alone in Room. After his birth, she had her child, the love of her life. Her priorities, her emotions, her minute-to-minute activities, center on him. Room itself is transformed. Instead of representing only her prison, she begins, for the sake of her son, to turn Room into a universe of possibilities.

Jack's fifth birthday acts as another defining moment. The predator Old Nick takes notice of Jack. For Joy, the status quo can no longer hold. Before Jack's birthday, Joy could protect Jack. After his birthday, Joy can no longer feel confident about keeping her child safe. Before this moment, Joy could keep her son at her side. After this moment, she knows she needs to send him away. As a consequence, this moment pushes Joy to take the most dangerous and extreme action of her years in captivity.

Jack and Joy's escape and reunion with Joy's parents represents another defining moment. Before the escape, they were prisoners under the power and control of Old Nick. After the escape, they are free. Before the escape, Joy's parents could only grieve the loss of their daughter and fear what had happened to her without any actual knowledge of her fate. After the escape, they can celebrate her return and fill the black hole in their knowledge of Joy's life all those years she was missing.

Each of these moments becomes a pivot point in the growth and transformation of the characters it touches. From point to point, we can track the way they change. These dramatic moments and the characters' responses to them make clear, visible, and comprehensible to the audience the characters' invisible inner journeys.

Where their journeys diverge, the defining moments help us understand why. Joy experiences not only the moment of her abduction and rape but also the moment of Jack's birth, along with all the changes his birth brings to her life. Joy's dad experiences the impact of his daughter's abduction but — and this is critical to understanding him — doesn't experience Jack's birth. Joy is redefined by Jack's presence. Her dad is not. As a consequence, Joy has an entirely different orientation toward Jack than does her dad. For Joy, Jack represents love and hope, informed by his presence in her life following his birth. For her dad, Jack represents only the horror and violence of the sole defining moment he experienced.

The inability of Joy's dad to keep up with his daughter's emotional growth because he missed pivotal moments of change — defining moments — mirrors the experience of the audience. We first watched *Room* as a screener, one of those DVDs the studios distribute during awards season to members of the various Hollywood guilds in hopes of encouraging nominations and awards. As we watched the unbearably intense sequence of Jack's escape and Joy's rescue, the DVD glitched and the movie froze. We stopped breathing. We stabbed buttons on the remote. We went apoplectic. You'd do the same.

When any one of us is caught up in a story, we can't bear to miss the defining moments. Not only do they make for riveting viewing, they make sense of the story. If the DVD skips, or if we race to the kitchen for a Hot Pocket, or if we need to slip out of our seat in the theater to visit the bathroom, and a defining moment takes place when we're not watching, we return to a character and a story we no longer understand. We weren't in the Winnebago when it made a sharp turn and drove off without us. When this happens, we will ask, often out loud, "What happened?!" Deprived of knowledge of their defining moments, we lose connection with our characters and their journeys.

Energizing the Performance of Actors Who've Come into Contact with the Deepest Forces Driving Their Characters

Do actors really think about where their characters come from and what has shaped them? Absolutely, says our friend Angie Bitsko, a veteran stage actor, director, and acting teacher in San Diego. "We're backstory-ing all the time."

But isn't "backstory-ing" the province of writers? Not at all, insists Bitsko. "I find that if actors just throw themselves into the script and into the story, it becomes very superficial. So you've got to step back, and you've got to figure out who you are, how you fit into the story, how you relate to the other characters. You're going to have to do a lot of work on your own."

Beyond figuring out relationships and a character's place in the story, Bitsko points to the specific value of an actor populating a character's backstory with pivotal moments not present in the script.

"We call it the actor's secret," says Bitsko. "There are going to be secrets that you have that aren't necessarily going to be shared with your audience, maybe even with other characters. It's those secrets, or defining moments, that shape and drive that character."

And the way Bitsko figures it, this work of creating robust backstories for characters doesn't belong only to leads and those playing featured characters. It may be even more important, she says, for ensemble characters. "As an actor, you don't want to be just a piece of furniture onstage. With enough audience members, someone is looking at you at every given moment." Her advice to every actor, no matter how many or few lines they have, even if the script refers to them as Soldier #2: "Give your character a name. That name may not appear on the marquee or in the program, but you know your name. You have a full life, and your life has significance."

When Bitsko directed a university production of the musical comedy *The Addams Family*, she tried an experiment. She challenged the actors to create full backstories for their characters, an assortment of dead relatives who come back in the present but who also share connections, along with pivotal moments — defining moments — from their pasts. Bitsko collected these stories of full, fleshed-out lives and created a family tree. "It's something the audience never saw," she recalls. "But onstage, that created a brand new dynamic. It fueled their energy as characters. It fueled the story with energy." How could it not? Every actor had discovered the engine that drove their character.

Equipping Writers, Directors, Actors, and All of Our Creative Collaborators as We Work Together Telling Deep, Honest, and Moving Stories

Look again at the restaurant scene from *The Godfather.** When he kills rival Sollozzo and police captain McCluskey, Michael

* For a more complete description of this moment, see the Introduction.

Corleone is going to cross a threshold from his old life into his new one. He will transform from upstanding citizen to crime boss, from innocent to killer. It's a passage that can't be reversed, a journey that can't be untraveled. Michael has passed a point of no return. This moment begins on the page, the work of an author and a screenwriter. In the screenplay, the heart of this decisive sequence, the actual moment when Michael flips the invisible internal switch that changes his inner moral landscape forever, takes place in the restaurant's bathroom. Michael has just found the gun that was planted for him in advance.

> CLOSE ON MICHAEL; the feel of it reassures him. Then he breaks it loose from the tape holding it; he takes a deep breath and shoves it under his waistband. For some unexplainable reason he hesitates once again, deliberately washes his hands and dries them. Then he goes out.*

Notice those words: "For some unexplainable reason he hesitates once again." They draw attention to this moment. They elongate it. They point to something "unexplainable," some important, unseen action. Then they give the actor something to do in this pause. He "washes his hands and dries them." Taken together, these words alert the actor, in this case Al Pacino, that important internal gears are turning. Then they give Pacino the time — "he hesitates once again" — and the action — "[he] deliberately washes his hands and dries them" — to play the life-altering internal turn. Here we have writers and actor working together to create a defining moment on the screen.

But those who remember this scene in detail know this isn't quite how the moment plays in the film. Here's what happens

---

* *The Godfather*, screenplay by Mario Puzo and Francis Ford Coppola, third draft, March 29, 1971, Paramount Pictures.

in the finished film after Michael finds the gun hidden behind the toilet tank. We cut back to the table where Sollozzo and McCluskey wait. McCluskey glances toward the bathroom, as if wondering what's taking Michael so long, heightening our sense of the passing time. Then we cut back to the bathroom, where Michael has already tucked the gun away, and we see him pass through one doorway, out of the toilet stall. The door swings closed behind him, but it's a door that only comes up to shoulder height so that we can see over the top of it. The camera holds, watching as Michael pauses between this door and the next — another shoulder-high door like the one on the toilet stall. He stands here and smooths his hair using both hands, holding his hands first over his face, then on the back of his neck, as if stuck in a moment of decision or commitment, just as he's stuck between the two doors. Then, the decision apparently made, Michael pushes through that next door, which swings closed behind him, and only then does he pass through a third door, this one the actual bathroom door that leads back into the restaurant, and finally pass from our view.

Here we see the work of Coppola wearing his director's hat. He recognized the importance of this moment to Michael's transformation. He recognized his need as a director to dramatize this invisible, internal movement in cinematic language so that he could photograph it and put it on the screen, unveiling it to the audience. He chose not to rely completely on that "unexplainable" hesitation and the extra handwashing to do the job. He staged and shot the moment using a sequence of three doors through which Michael must pass, and he had Pacino pause between those doors. It's in that freighted visual space that Pacino's performance externalizes his inner moment of commitment to the action he's about to take.

Who created this defining moment onscreen? A novelist. A screenwriting team. A director. Three actors. A production designer. A cinematographer. And an editor. Not to mention a sound designer, a composer, a dozen or so extras, and an army of others who recognized the towering importance of this moment not only to the plot but to the character of Michael Corleone. They each brought their specialized storytelling powers to bear to create this scene, which runs over eight minutes in total, lingers in the minds of the audience, and undergirds everything that follows in this film and its sequels.

Actor Joseph Barone observes that different members of the creative team sometimes use different terms to describe the storytelling dynamics with which they engage. "To me, it's always valuable when you're able to match those terms to anyone you're working with, be that an actor or, even better, a director, or even a writer, if you have that opportunity to know where they were coming from when creating the character. And also learning [from the way they speak about their work], going, 'Ooh, I like that better. I actually like how you as a writer would say this, and I'm going to steal that now.' It's more active for me. It's more interesting. It makes me more interesting on camera."

Creating defining moments, it turns out, is a team sport. Writers, directors, and actors lead the way. Our collaborators eagerly join us, storytellers all. For each of us, our storytelling instincts recognize and home in on these moments like heatseeking missiles.

* * *

Storytellers who understand and employ the dynamic power of

defining moments will charge their stories with emotion, deepen the investment of the audience in their characters, reveal their characters' growth, and focus the extraordinary abilities of their collaborators to create moments that will keep all of our eyes glued to the screen.

How do writers, directors, and actors recognize defining moments and harness their extraordinary power to its fullest? They can begin by grasping the range of the various sorts of moments that can define characters. In Chapter 2, we'll examine the characteristics of a wide spectrum of defining moments.

2.
Characteristics of Defining Moments

THE DAY OUR MENTOR COLEMAN LUCK INTRODUCED US TO THE CONCEPT of defining moments, we hadn't yet experienced the wrenching event that created our family's starkest boundary of before and after. We hadn't yet crossed the threshold from which there could be no return to the life we'd been living.

Our son Peter was five years old. He was a red-haired imp, a jokester, confident and sociable. Rachel, our daughter, was eight. She relished her role as big sister and choreographed elaborate dance routines that she and Peter performed to Céline Dion tunes.

One day, Chris accompanied Peter to preschool for a take-your-parent-to-school day. Chris, an introvert unsure about what sorts of interactions this event would entail, told Peter he was a little nervous about the whole thing. Peter rolled his eyes. His voice dripping with condescension, he said, "Dad, it's only preschool." Apart from his son's rebuke, what Chris later most vividly recalled from that day was the sidebar conversation he had with one of

Peter's teachers, who confided, no doubt violating every norm of responsible teaching, that Peter was the smartest kid in the preschool.

Once, as Kathy sat in the rocking chair in our living room cradling Peter on her lap, she told Chris she feared her sweet son was too good for this world.

Maybe it was Peter's round angelic face that gave rise to Kathy's anxiety. Or maybe it was the series of doctor's appointments to which we'd taken him, trying to understand why he'd begun suffering headaches, some of which became so severe he would vomit until he eventually found relief in sleep.

These were the days when we were putting the finishing touches on *After the Truth*, the screenplay we were rewriting under Luck's tutelage. We'd done the character work our mentor demanded. We'd excavated our hero Peter Rohm's past and present and discovered the moments that defined him. We'd worked some of those moments into this new draft of the script. On a Thursday, we polished a line of dialogue for Rohm, a German attorney, part of his climactic closing argument in the trial of Josef Mengele. The rewritten line crescendoed, improbably enough, with reference to a five-year-old getting cancer. On Friday morning, our five-year-old son, as part of our ongoing quest to learn the cause of his headaches, went into an MRI scanner. Before the afternoon ended, we stood in a hallway in the emergency department at UCLA Medical Center looking at black and white images of what the neurosurgeon explained was an "impressive tumor" in our son's brain.

Many years later, every member of our family looks back on that moment as one that marks a boundary we crossed from before to after. We speak of the time "before Peter got sick." And we speak of the time "after Peter's brain tumor." We recognize that each of our lives changed as a result of that moment. Some of those changes were grievous. Others turned out to be beautiful. For years after the surgery, we fought to get back to the lives we'd had before that moment of diagnosis. We fought with radiation and chemotherapy and transfusions and feeding tubes. We fought with occupational therapy, with physical therapy, with play therapy. We fought with all our hearts. Peter fought with all his strength. But it was impossible. There was no going back. There was only moving forward, moving away from the boy Peter had been, away from the people we had been, away from the lives we'd been living, into something new and forever changed.

This is the nature of defining moments. All such moments create turning points, moments that, for a given character, divide before from after. As storytellers, this quality helps us recognize our characters' defining moments. It helps us craft these moments. And it helps us bring them into focus for the audience.

What other qualities distinguish these moments? Understanding their common traits will help us recognize, craft, and present them as we deepen and enrich our characters.

By paying attention over the years to defining moments that show up in literature and on the stage and screen, we've observed that beyond the universal quality of dividing before from after, defining moments almost always share one or more of the following characteristics:

- A grievous loss is suffered.
- A lasting wound is inflicted.
- A deep and lasting emotional change occurs.
- A moral or spiritual change takes place.
- A life-changing choice is made.
- A life-changing discovery is made.
- A profound lesson is learned.
- A birth or death occurs.

- A connection or commitment is made or broken.
- A dream or longing is awakened.
- Healing or growth takes place.

Each of these characteristics deserves closer examination.

A Grievous Loss Is Suffered

Loss holds a unique power to shape us. We may lose a person, as Forrest Gump loses Jenny to death in the defining moment that takes place near the end of his film. We may lose a place, as the villagers of Anatevka are forced from their homes in a defining moment at the mournful climax of *Fiddler on the Roof*. We may lose a possession, as Sauron loses the ring to Isildur in the opening battle scene of *The Lord of the Rings: The Fellowship of the Ring*— and as Gollum loses the same ring to Bilbo in *The Hobbit*. We may lose a dream, as each member of the Younger family does in *A Raisin in the Sun* when Walter loses the life insurance money on which all of their dreams depend.

The loss of someone or something of great value may result in lingering grief. The pain resulting from a deep loss, such as the loss of a child, may persist for a lifetime and inform every subsequent emotional experience and every subsequent choice a character makes. Because this is the case, how can we understand such a character if we remain ignorant of their loss? Loss can change a character profoundly.

A moment of loss may provide a character's motivation to act. Sauron, after losing the ring to Isildur, is driven by a longing to regain his lost treasure, the key to the power he craves. Once Gollum has lost the ring to Bilbo, he can think of nothing but getting back "my precious," as he calls it. The combat deaths of three out of four Ryan brothers early in *Saving Private Ryan* represent such a great loss that it moves even the U.S. Army in the most desperate days of World War II to dispatch a rescue mission to bring back the surviving brother.

A moment of loss may shape a character's behavior. A character may habitually take refuge in denial that the loss has been suffered. Or a character may engage in a strategy of self-protection to guard against further loss, as Marlin does in *Finding Nemo*.

A moment of loss may fuel a quest for justice or revenge. In *Just Mercy*, attorney Bryan Stevenson responds to his client Walter McMillian's loss of liberty and wrongful incarceration on death row by pursuing a years-long quest for justice. In *Gladiator,* Roman general Maximus suffers the loss of his family, his freedom, and the emperor he serves at the hands of Commodus, the emperor's murderous son. Maximus becomes a gladiator with the abiding goal of avenging his terrible losses.

A moment of loss may result in a character's growth. Characters who suffer loss may grow in compassion, wisdom, humility, or generosity. In the climactic battle near the end of *The Lord of the Rings: The Fellowship of the Ring*, the warrior Boromir loses his life after attempting to take the ring from Frodo in a moment of hubris and folly, but in the process, he gains humility and wisdom. In the 1991 film *The Doctor*, William Hurt plays Dr. Jack McKee, a carelessly arrogant and insensitive surgeon who seems to have skipped the med school class on bedside manner. Then Dr. McKee comes down with cancer and becomes a patient in his own hospital. He suffers the loss of his health and of the fiction that he is somehow insulated from the sicknesses he treats. Those losses change McKee. He grows in compassion. His approach to his patients is transformed. So is the way he trains his students. And none of that transformation could have happened without his defining moment of loss.

A Lasting Wound Is Inflicted

Can the infliction of a wound exert similar character-defining force? Consider the classic tale *Peter Pan.* Peter cuts off Captain James Hook's hand and feeds it to a crocodile in a moment that permanently disfigures Hook, gives new meaning to his name, instills his fear of the crocodile that forever after pursues him, and supercharges his own drive to avenge himself on Peter.

Soon after Frodo Baggins, in *The Lord of the Rings*, sets out from Bree with his companion hobbits and the mysterious ranger he knows only as Strider, he suffers a lasting wound at a place called Weathertop. There, the Dark Riders, servants of the dark lord Sauron, attack Frodo and the other hobbits by night. Before Strider can drive the attackers away, one of these ghostly former "kings of men," the Witch-king of Angmar, plunges his sword into Frodo's shoulder. Gravely wounded, Frodo only survives with the help of the elves. But even after Frodo recovers, he carries with him a permanent scar and lasting pain. And his wound from this Morgul blade changes him in deeper ways, making him less carefree and more attuned to life's dangers and evils, haunting him with a degree of sadness and making him unfit to remain long in the Shire even after his quest to destroy the ring is done.

For both Captain Hook and Frodo, the moments they receive a lasting wound become moments that define them.

Examples of the defining power of a wound appear not only in modern storytelling but in ancient literature. In an account recorded in the Biblical Book of Genesis, the patriarch Jacob is returning from years in exile after cheating his older brother Esau out of his inheritance and fleeing for his life. Now, many years later, Jacob is journeying back to his homeland with the wives, children, and massive flocks he has accumulated while in exile. As he nears the old family home, he receives word that Esau is marching toward him with four hundred armed men.

Jacob is terrified. He fears his brother intends to exact revenge. To appease his estranged brother's anger, Jacob organizes extravagant gifts for Esau from his flocks. Jacob sends those gifts, along with everyone in his traveling party, ahead of him, while Jacob himself remains behind. Jacob spends the night before he will meet Esau and his army in terrible anticipation. And during that dreadful night, he encounters a deeply mysterious character whom the millennia-old text initially identifies as "a man" but whom Jacob later recognizes as God. Genesis reports that Jacob wrestles with this "man" until daybreak, at which point the man inflicts a lasting injury to Jacob's hip and gives Jacob a new name, Israel. The moment of wounding recounted by this story changes Jacob, giving him a new identity. Thousands of years later, that name still appears on world maps, an enduring appellation bestowed alongside an enduring wound.

Forrest Gump's Lieutenant Dan Taylor suffers a life-altering injury fighting in the jungles of Vietnam. Despite Taylor's demand that Forrest leave him to die, Forrest carries his platoon leader to safety. For years thereafter, Lieutenant Dan responds to his wound with anger and self-pity. He rages against Forrest for rescuing him, cheating him out of the noble death he believes was his destiny, and leaving him instead to live life as a double-amputee, dependent on a wheelchair for mobility. Over time, Taylor's anger ripens, until, as a hurricane rages in the Gulf of Mexico, his wound motivates a shouting match aboard the shrimping boat *Jenny* between him and God. So changed is this character after the storm that he thanks Forrest for saving his life. Forrest says of his former platoon leader, "He never actually said so, but I think he made his peace with God." Even more years later, Lieutenant Dan shows up at the wedding of Forrest and Jenny, accompanied by a wife of his own and walking on prosthetics that Forrest dubs his "magic legs," signaling that the internal aspect of the wound has at last healed.

The audience tracks Lieutenant Dan's character arc through three defining moments. The first is the moment he loses his legs. The second is the moment during the hurricane when he airs his grievances with God. And the third is the moment he finds new legs and the love of his wife. Each is a dramatic moment of change. Taken together, they dramatize a character's journey of transformation.

Sometimes, a character can suffer a wound that is more complex and subtler than we might ever imagine.

Nobel laureate Toni Morrison used her first novel, *The Bluest Eye*, to explore the nature and impact of a lasting wound on her main character, a young black girl named Pecola Breedlove who wishes for blue eyes. In her introduction to the 1970 novel, Morrison describes the link she wanted to explore between Pecola's unique inner wound and the series of events — at least some of them what we might call defining moments — that inflicted it:

> The extremity of Pecola's case stemmed largely from a crippled and crippling family — unlike the average black family and unlike the narrator's. But singular as Pecola's life was, I believed some aspects of her woundability were lodged in all young girls. In exploring the social and domestic aggression that could cause a child to literally fall apart, I mounted a series of rejections, some routine, some exceptional, some monstrous.*

The story takes place in the 1940s in Morrison's hometown of Lorain, Ohio, where young Pecola grows up in an abusive home. The author reveals early in the novel Pecola's scandalous condition:

> Quiet as it's kept, there were no marigolds in the fall of 1941.

---

* Toni Morrison, *The Bluest Eye*, Vintage International, 1970.

> We thought, at the time, that it was because Pecola was having her father's baby that the marigolds did not grow . . . It was a long time before my sister and I admitted to ourselves that no green was going to spring from our seeds . . . We had dropped our seeds in our own little plot of black dirt just as Pecola's father had dropped his seeds in his own plot of black dirt. Our innocence and faith were no more productive than his lust or despair. What is clear now is that of all of that hope, fear, lust, love, and grief, nothing remains but Pecola and the unyielding earth. Cholly Breedlove is dead; our innocence too. The seeds shriveled and died; her baby too.
>
> There is really nothing more to say — except why. But since *why* is difficult to handle, one must take refuge in *how*.

The remainder of the novel explores the how. It tells the how for Pecola and the how for her friends Frieda and Claudia, who suffer a different sort of wound than Pecola but are permanently altered nonetheless. Claudia, the novel's narrator, describes how she came to know the story of Pecola's situation by overhearing neighbors gossip about Pecola, her father, and the baby growing inside the tiny girl.

> "She be lucky if it don't live. Bound to be the ugliest thing walking."
>
> "Can't help but be. Ought to be a law: two ugly people doubling up like that to make more ugly. Be better off in the ground."
>
> "Well, I wouldn't worry none. It be a miracle if it live."
>
> Our astonishment was short-lived, for it gave way to a curious kind of defensive shame; we were embarrassed for Pecola, hurt for her, and finally we just felt sorry for her . . . And I believe our sorrow was the more intense because nobody else

> seemed to share it . . . More strongly than my fondness for Pecola, I felt a need for someone to want the black baby to live — just to counteract the universal love of white baby dolls, Shirley Temples, and Maureen Peals.

Sisters Frieda and Claudia make a deal with God. They will give up the money they've saved to buy a bicycle and will plant the marigold seeds they've been selling to earn the money if God will keep Pecola's baby alive.

The baby comes too soon, however, and dies.

Claudia describes the effect of these events on Pecola, and on herself and her sister:

> The damage done was total. She spent her days, her tendril, sap-green days, walking up and down, up and down, her head jerking to the beat of a drummer so distant only she could hear. Elbows bent, hands on shoulders, she flailed her arms like a bird in an eternal, grotesquely futile effort to fly. Beating the air, a winged but grounded bird, intent on the blue void it could not reach — could not even see — but which filled the valleys of the mind.
>
> We tried to see her without looking at her, and never, never went near. Not because she was absurd, or repulsive, or because we were frightened, but because we had failed her. Our flowers never grew. I was convinced that Frieda was right, that I had planted them too deeply. How could I have been so sloven? So we avoided Pecola Breedlove — forever.
>
> And the years folded up like pocket handkerchiefs . . . And Pecola is somewhere in that little brown house she and her mother moved to on the edge of town, where you can see her even now, once in a while. The birdlike gestures are worn away to a mere picking and plucking her way between the tire rims

> and the sunflowers, between Coke bottles and milkweed, among all the waste and beauty of the world — which is what she herself was. All of our waste which we dumped on her and which she absorbed. And all of our beauty, which was hers first and which she gave to us. All of us — all who knew her — felt so wholesome after we cleaned ourselves on her. We were so beautiful when we stood astride her ugliness. Her simplicity decorated us, her guilt sanctified us, her pain made us glow with health . . . Even her waking dreams we used — to silence our own nightmares. And she let us, and thereby deserved our contempt. We honed our egos on her, padded our characters with her frailty, and yawned in the fantasy of our strength.

The wound lays waste to Pecola. Perversely, it fills Frieda and Claudia with confidence in a strength and goodness they don't possess. Their wound, though pernicious, is invisible, even to them.

How public and devastating a wound can be. And how subtle and complex.

A Deep and Lasting Emotional Change Occurs

Sometimes, the impact of an experience reverberates through a permanent emotional change in a character, for better or for worse. When young Bruce Wayne witnesses the murder of his parents, he undergoes this sort of lasting emotional change. In the pilot script for the series *Gotham*, writer Bruno Heller introduces the boy Bruce and his parents walking through an alley, "laughing" and talking "lightly" with one another after a night at the movies. They're confronted by a masked robber with a gun. Heller writes, "Bruce is terrified." After Bruce's mother and father hand over their valuables, the gunman shoots them anyway, then puts his gun to Bruce's head before lowering the weapon and walking away.

"Frozen in horror," the script tells us, "Bruce watches his mother and father trying to speak, gasping for their last breaths in a spreading pool of blood."

The boy tries to speak to them. "Mom? Dad?"

But it's too late. Bruce falls to his knees and, in the words of the script, lets out "an UNEARTHLY WAIL."

The next time we see Bruce, the police have arrived, and Bruce is "sitting on a doorstep, wrapped in a police department blanket, his face a mask of tragedy," feeling what Heller describes as "fathomless pain."

Detective Gordon questions Bruce, who confesses, "I could have grabbed the gun. But I didn't. I didn't do anything."

When Gordon assures Bruce he did the right thing, Bruce disagrees. "No. I should have done something. I was too scared."

Gordon responds, "There was nothing you could do to stop what happened. But there is something you can do now. Now you can be strong. Grief can make you strong. Be strong and one day maybe you can stop this from happening to somebody else."

Heller writes, "Bruce nods. Gordon has no idea how deep his words sink in."

Much like the writers of *Finding Nemo*, the writer of *Gotham* begins his story with a moment of deep and lasting emotional change for one of its central characters. At this pivotal moment, Bruce's emotional state changes from lightness to enduring grief. Darkness falls over the boy. In addition, Bruce Wayne begins his journey from fear and weakness to a strength that will emerge with a singular aim: "Be strong and one day maybe you can stop this from happening to somebody else." Notice that Heller, in order to emphasize the deep and lasting nature of this emotional change, writes for the benefit of actor and director alike, "Gordon has no idea how deep his words sink in."

If we don't know about this moment early in Bruce Wayne's life, we don't know Bruce Wayne. It's the moment that defines him as the Dark Knight.

In the landmark television series *Breaking Bad*, protagonist Walter White undergoes a dramatic emotional makeover. In Vince Gilligan's pilot script, we meet Walter as a meek, emasculated high school chemistry teacher sleepwalking through life. But soon after he receives a cancer diagnosis and the prospect of no more than two years to live, he makes a life-changing decision. Executing a sharp turn away from the shell of a human he's become, he joins forces with Jesse Pinkman, a ne'er-do-well former student turned meth dealer. Walt intends to use his own expertise in chemistry to cook New Mexico's purest methamphetamine and, in his dying days, use Pinkman's knowledge of drug dealing to secure his family's financial future.

As Walt and Pinkman gather the money to buy a Winnebago they plan to use as a mobile meth lab, the baffled Pinkman says to his former teacher, "You're not how I remember you from class. I mean, like, not at all." Pinkman insists, "Tell me why you're doing this. Seriously."

Walt takes a beat, then turns the question around on Pinkman. "Why do you do it?"

"Money, mainly," says Pinkman.

"There you have it."

"Nah. Come on, man! Some straight like you, giant stick up his ass . . . all of a sudden at age, what, fifty he's just gonna break bad?"

"I'm forty-one."

Pinkman presses. "It's weird, is all. It doesn't compute. If you're like . . . crazy or something . . . if you've gone crazy, or depressed. I'm just saying. That's something I need to know about. That affects me."

Walt stares at Pinkman a long time, Gilligan writes, as he considers how to answer. When Walt next speaks, he gives voice in three simple words to the profound emotional change he's just undergone, a change that represents the key to understanding his decisions and actions for the remaining six seasons.

"I am . . . awake."

With those three words, the protagonist of *Breaking Bad* describes his transformation. Without comprehending the defining moment that effected Walt's dramatic emotional change, this character remains an enigma. But understanding this moment unlocks the mystery of Walter White.

A final memorable example of the way defining moments can effect a deep and enduring emotional change in a character comes from the 2005 film *Finding Neverland*, adapted to the screen by David Magee from a play by Allan Knee. In this film, Johnny Depp plays J.M. Barrie, playwright and creator of the iconic character Peter Pan and the fantasy world Neverland, where boys never grow up. Over time, the term "Peter Pan syndrome" has understandably attached to people, especially men, who fail to take on the responsibilities of adulthood. This phenomenon can lead us to dismiss the character of Peter Pan and the playwright who conceived him as belonging to a class of immature, commitment-averse, responsibility-dodging shirkers. But Magee's Oscar-nominated screenplay shines a spotlight on a defining moment in Barrie's childhood that transforms our understanding of the real reason Barrie conceived the character of Peter Pan and the realm of Neverland. When we hear Barrie describe the moment, we're struck by the before-and-after quality of the experience and the starkness of the emotional change it wrought in him. And we see in this moment the seeds of both Peter Pan and Neverland.

In the film, Depp's Barrie movingly describes the moment that changed him in a conversation with his widowed friend Sylvia, played in the film by Kate Winslet, who happens to have a young son named Peter.

"You mean a lot to my boys, you know," Sylvia says to Barrie. "Especially Peter."

Barrie replies, "It seems to me that Peter's trying to grow up too fast. I imagine he thinks that grown-ups don't hurt as deeply as children do when they . . . when they lose someone."

After making this astute but rather generic observation, Barrie makes a far more specific and personal disclosure, revealing a moment from his past.

"I lost my elder brother, David," he says, "when I was just Peter's age. And it nearly destroyed my mother."

"James, I'm so sorry. Your poor mother. I can't imagine losing a child," says Sylvia.

"Aye. She didn't get out of bed for months. She wouldn't eat. I tried everything to make her happy, but . . . she only wanted David. So . . . one day . . . I dressed myself in David's clothing and I went to her."

"You must have frightened her to death."

"I think it was the first time she ever actually . . . looked at me. And that was the end of the boy James."

You can picture the boy James in that moment crossing the threshold from childhood into adulthood, a moment of before and after. And you can wrap your heart around the profound emotional change that resulted. Understanding that moment casts Barrie and his creations Peter Pan and Neverland in an entirely new and far more sympathetic light.

In each instance, for Bruce Wayne and Walter White and J.M. Barrie, a deep and lasting emotional change occurs in a moment that defines these iconic characters.

A Moral or Spiritual Change Takes Place

In other instances, the defining change isn't emotional. Instead, it's moral or spiritual. Recall the case of *The Godfather*'s Michael Corleone. When Michael kills Sollozzo, the rival crime boss, and McCluskey, the corrupt police captain, he crosses a line that separates the innocent from the guilty, the law-abiding from the criminal. That line can't be uncrossed. The change to Michael is more than technical or legal. It's moral and spiritual. In that defining moment in the restaurant, Michael embraces a darkness and violence that will corrode his soul and lead him to greater and uglier acts of destruction. To understand that years-long spiritual descent, we must understand the moment it began and the impact it had on Michael's soul.

In contrast to this light-into-darkness transition, *Spider-Man 2*'s antagonist experiences a defining moment in which he steps out of darkness into light. The supervillain of that film, written by Alvin Sargent from a story by Alfred Gough, Miles Millar, and Michael Chabon, is Dr. Otto Octavius. In a defining moment early in the film, grief-stricken at the death of his wife and determined to exact revenge on those he blames, Octavius gives into the corrupting power of AI-assisted mechanical tentacles of his own creation. This move mirrors that of *The Godfather*'s Michael Corleone and Tolkien's Gollum. But it's the defining moment that comes at the climax of the film that demonstrates an additional possibility. Spider-Man confronts Octavius at his waterfront lab as Octavius revs up a nuclear-powered experiment that will destroy New York. Spider-Man appeals to the humanity he hopes remains buried somewhere inside Octavius. The supervillain responds to his appeal, resisting the insidious power that has mastered him and sacrificing himself to destroy his experiment and save the city. In doing so, he reconnects with a measure of his own humanity in a way that feels thoroughly moral. In that defining moment, though Octavius dies, he seems to pass from darkness back into light.

In literature, such moments predate *Spider-Man 2* by millennia. For a centuries-old example, consider Shakespeare's Macbeth and Lady Macbeth. Like Michael Corleone, they choose to murder a rival in power, King Duncan. That murder changes them at some spiritual level that leads them deeper into darkness. They kill again and again until, at last, Macbeth himself is slain and fear and guilt consume Lady Macbeth.

For a more hopeful example, we can leap forward to the nineteenth century and Charles Dickens' *A Christmas Carol* to witness the redemption of the heartless miser Ebenezer Scrooge. Over the course of a single Christmas Eve, the Ghosts of Christmas Past, Present, and Future confront the greedy old banker. His experience that night offers him an opportunity to alter the shape of his soul. In a spectacular moment of before and after, we see him escape a moral and spiritual black hole of greed and bitterness and emerge onto a bright new path marked by generosity and joy.

A Life-Changing Choice Is Made

We've previously noted that Robert McKee, in his book *Story*, points to the significance of the choices characters make under pressure. These choices, McKee argues, reveal true character. Is it possible that choice can also redefine, i.e. change, that inner nature?

Early in James Cameron's 1997 epic action-romance *Titanic*, Kate Winslet's character Rose, a young British aristocrat trapped in an unhappy engagement, makes her way to the stern of the ship as it steams across the North Atlantic. So great is her despair in this instant, she climbs onto the railing and gazes down into the icy water, preparing to jump. Jack Dawson, a free-spirited American artist, sees this tragedy unfolding and intervenes. In Cameron's screenplay, the moment plays out like this:

> Moving methodically she turns her body and gets her heels on the white-painted gunwale, her back to the railing, facing out toward blackness. 60 feet below her, the massive propellers are churning the Atlantic into white foam, and a ghostly wake trails off toward the horizon.
>
> IN A LOW ANGLE, we see Rose standing like a figurehead in reverse. Below her are the huge letters of the name "TITANIC."
>
> She leans out, her arms straightening . . . looking down hypnotized, into the vortex below her. Her dress and hair are lifted by the wind of the ship's movement. The only sound, above the rush of water below, is the flutter and snap of the big Union Jack right above her.
>
> JACK: Don't do it.
>
> She whips her head around at the sound of his voice. It takes a second for her eyes to focus.
>
> ROSE: Stay back! Don't come any closer!
>
> Jack sees the tear tracks on her cheeks in the faint glow from the stern running lights.
>
> JACK: Take my hand. I'll pull you back in.
>
> ROSE: No! Stay where you are. I mean it. I'll let go.

In the film, Jack proceeds to explain to Rose that if she jumps, he'll have to leap in after her. As he removes his jacket and shoes, he describes the knifelike pain he anticipates they'll both suffer in the icy water. But he makes clear that she'll leave him no choice. If she jumps, his honor will compel him to jump. The scene continues:

> JACK: I'm kinda hoping you'll come back over the rail and get me off the hook here.
>
> ROSE: You're crazy.
>
> JACK: That's what everybody says. But with all due respect, I'm not the one hanging off the back of a ship.
>
> He slides one step closer, like moving up on a spooked horse.
>
> JACK: Come on. You don't want to do this. Give me your hand.
>
> Rose stares at this madman for a long time. She looks at his eyes and they somehow suddenly seem to fill her universe.
>
> ROSE: Alright.
>
> She unfastens one hand from the rail and reaches it around toward him. He reaches out to take it, firmly.
>
> JACK: I'm Jack Dawson.
>
> ROSE (voice quavering): Pleased to meet you, Mr. Dawson.
>
> Rose starts to turn. Now that she has decided to live, the height is terrifying.

"Now that she has decided to live," writes Cameron. She's made a choice, and suddenly everything is different. Before she made her decision to live, the nearness of death felt inviting, intoxicating, seductive. Now, it terrifies.

Rose decides to live. That moment on the stern of the doomed ocean liner becomes a turning point for her. Instead of ending her life that night, she begins a fight to survive the oppression of her social circumstances, soon fights a harrowing battle to survive the sinking ship, and finally goes on to live another eighty-four rich, full years. And it all hinges on a choice she makes in a defining moment.

The fate of Frodo Baggins and of all Middle Earth turns on another character choice. At the midpoint of *The Fellowship of the Ring*, the first film of the *Lord of the Rings* trilogy, the hobbit Frodo has arrived in Rivendell, home of the elves. Here he recuperates from the wound he received on Weathertop when his shoulder was pierced by the Witch-king's Morgul blade. As he mends, Lord Elrond, chief of the elves, summons a secret council of leading elves, dwarves, hobbits, wizards, and men. They have to make a decision on which hangs the fate of their world, Tolkien's Middle Earth. Now that Frodo has delivered to them the One Ring, a token invested with formidable power, they must decide what to do with it. Some want to destroy it on the spot, lest it fall into the hands of the Dark Lord Sauron and enable him to extend his evil rule over them all. They discover, however, that they don't possess the power to destroy the ring. It can only be destroyed, Elrond tells them, by casting it into the fires of Mount Doom in the heart of Mordor, the realm of the Dark Lord. The human warrior Boromir argues that they should use the ring themselves, harnessing its power for good, enabling them to defeat Sauron in battle. This, advises Elrond, is also impossible. Though any one of them would intend to use the power of the ring for good, its power would corrupt them, and they would in the end fall under its seductive sway. The only option is for one of them to carry the ring through Mordor to Mount Doom and cast it into the fire burning inside that mountain, thus destroying the ring and dissolving its power.

Frodo watches as the council erupts in a chaos of argument and accusation. The power of the ring seems already to be working its will, setting the members of the council at one another's throats. In this moment of bitter contention, the diminutive hobbit makes a decision.

He rises and announces, "I will take it."

As Frodo steps forward and repeats his pledge, the old wizard Gandalf lowers his gaze, understanding what this choice will almost certainly cost Frodo.

"I will take the ring to Mordor," says Frodo, silencing the astonished councilors. "Though," he allows, "I do not know the way."

This moment of decision for Frodo becomes a defining moment for him, for the fellowship of eight companions who pledge their lives to see him complete his quest, and for every resident of Middle Earth whose happiness and survival depend on his success.

Shakespeare, like Tolkien, harnessed the power of character choices. During the first act of his revered play *Hamlet*, Shakespeare confronts his title character with an almost impossible dilemma. On the ramparts of Elsinore, the castle of Denmark's royal household, Prince Hamlet encounters an apparition who claims to be the ghost of his dead father. The ghost tells Hamlet that he was murdered by his brother, Claudius, Hamlet's uncle, who has since married Hamlet's mother and taken the throne. The ghost orders Hamlet to avenge his murder by killing Claudius.

Hamlet must decide. Will he kill King Claudius on the word of a ghost? Will he instead disbelieve and defy the ghost, and let Claudius live? Unwilling to commit to either of these options — in effect, refusing to make the decision forced upon him by the ghost — Hamlet quickly chooses a third way. He decides to act as if he's lost his mind, hoping to tease out the truth of what role Claudius may have played in the death of his father. From this choice flows the rest of the story. And from this choice flows almost endless tragedy and death. The bloody climax at the end of the final act of *Hamlet* results from the defining moment of Hamlet's choice in the first act.

A Life-Changing Discovery Is Made

Characters often make life-changing choices only after making a life-changing discovery. Remember the milquetoast high school chemistry teacher Walter White, the protagonist of the series *Breaking Bad*? He chose to use his chemistry skills to begin manufacturing meth only after receiving the news that he had terminal lung cancer. His discovery of his imminent death primed Walt for his choice to restyle himself as an outlaw.

In the pilot episode of the long-running series *The Walking Dead*, lead character Rick Grimes, a deputy sheriff in a small Georgia town, awakens in his local hospital days after being shot by a fugitive only to discover that while he was unconscious the world had turned upside down. The flowers beside his bed have wilted. The medical staff have abandoned the hospital. Bodies litter the corridors. And behind a chained door painted with the chilling warning "Dead Inside," something moves. Human arms, dead or alive, or something neither dead nor alive, reach through a gap between the doors, clawing to break free. Rick finds dozens more bodies stacked outside the hospital. On a nearby hill, he finds a military camp that appears to have been overrun by some bloodthirsty enemy force. He makes his way home and finds that his family is missing. Only the dead seem to populate the world. But these dead move. They walk. They hunt. They feed. Rick's discovery that these "walkers" have overrun his town and killed or scattered everyone he knows and loves becomes a dramatic defining moment, demarcating before from after, spinning his life and story in a radical new direction.

A Profound Lesson Is Learned

In the classic 1939 musical *The Wizard of Oz*, Dorothy makes a discovery that falls into a special category. She discovers a truth. She learns a lesson. After chafing at her small and confined life on

Auntie Em's Kansas farm and running away to seek something better, Dorothy learns there's no place like home. The discovery of that truth, the learning of that lesson, represents a distinct step of growth for Dorothy. The mantra "There's no place like home" becomes the key to her return to the farm and to her appreciation of the people she had earlier abandoned as too ordinary to cherish. That moment of lesson-learning becomes a turning point in Dorothy's life and a moment that defines her.

A Birth or Death Occurs

So pivotal are moments of birth and death to us culturally, we find them at the center of many of our national and religious holidays.

- The Fourth of July commemorates the birth of the United States, the date Americans declared independence from the English king, George III.
- Presidents' Day celebrates the birthdays of U.S. Presidents George Washington and Abraham Lincoln.
- Martin Luther King Jr. Day marks the birthday of civil rights leader Martin Luther King Jr.
- Memorial Day and 9/11, or Patriot Day, remember U.S. military members who have died in service to their country and those who died in the terror attacks of 2001, respectively.
- Juneteenth recalls the day in June of 1865 when news of the end of the Civil War and of Abraham Lincoln's two-and-a-half-year-old Emancipation Proclamation reached enslaved people in Galveston, Texas, marking the death of slavery in the United States and the birth of a long and halting march toward freedom.
- The Hindu holiday Krishna Janmashtami celebrates the birth of Krishna.

- For Muslims, Mawlid celebrates the birth of Muhammad.
- The Jewish holiday of Passover remembers the deliverance — a kind of birth — of the Jewish people from bondage in Egypt in an event involving the death of countless Passover lambs and the firstborn of Egypt.
- Three major Christian holidays, Christmas, Good Friday, and Easter, celebrate the birth, death, and resurrection, a kind of rebirth, of Jesus.

And year after year, we celebrate our own births and the births of those we love with parties and cards and gifts, just as we often and in a variety of different ways mark the anniversaries of the deaths of those we've loved.

The beloved 1993 romantic comedy *Sleepless in Seattle* stars Tom Hanks as Sam and Meg Ryan as Annie, an architect and a journalist living in distant cities who, we are led to believe, are destined to find love and happiness together. But in addition to living hundreds of miles apart and never having met, they're already in love with other people. Annie is engaged to marry a smart, sensitive man with impressive allergies. Sam is more-than-happily married to Maggie, Sam's soulmate and the mother of the couple's cherubic son, Jonah. Nothing in their lives is pointing Sam and Annie toward romance with one another.

And then Sam's wife Maggie dies.

This is the moment writers Nora Ephron, David S. Ward, and Jeff Arch choose to begin the film. It's a defining moment for Sam, ending his happy marriage, plunging him into grief, turning him into a single parent, and sending him and young Jonah to start a new life in Seattle. When Jonah persuades Sam to tell the story of this moment on a national radio call-in show, Annie hears it, she's smitten, and the trajectory of her life changes. The movie's plot, character arcs, theme, and emotional tone all depend on the existence of this moment.

Pixar's 2009 film *Up* begins with a moving visual sequence that tells the love story of Carl and Ellie. The sequence consists of a series of defining moments from their relationship and culminates with the moment that informs both Carl's emotional state and his motivation for the remainder of the movie: the moment of his beloved Ellie's death.

In the film *Room*, it's not death but the birth of the son of captive teen Joy Newsome that reframes her identity and redefines her life. At the moment of her son Jack's birth, Joy transitions from years of forced isolation to a life of treasured companionship, from child to parent, from passive victim to driven protagonist. Joy recognizes the transformative impact of this moment in her life and ritualizes the telling of its story so that it becomes a memory she and Jack share and celebrate. The first words uttered by a character in the film consist, in fact, of Jack reciting this shared story.

> JACK (V.O.): You cried all day and left TV on till you were a zombie. But then I zoomed down from heaven through Skylight into Room — (makes noise of descent, then crash landing) and I was kicking you from the inside, boom boom, and then I shot out onto Rug with my eyes wide open, and you cutted the cord and said "Hello Jack."

Not coincidentally, the film begins on Jack's fifth birthday. The commemoration of the defining moment of his birth becomes a defining moment of its own, a moment that catalyzes Joy's urgent quest to deliver Jack yet again, this time into the world beyond the walls of the backyard shed that imprisons them.

A Connection or Commitment Is Made or Broken

In her revelatory book *Crafting Short Screenplays That Connect*, author Claudia Hunter Johnson highlights the power of connections and disconnections within and between characters to imbue cinematic moments with emotion. She writes:

> There are moments of change in our lives and stories that are not comprehended by conflict. These moments of change are connections, human exchanges, however fleeting or small . . . Connection is human sustenance, the substance of story. Its gain and loss provide the emotional power.*

Recall the moment young Forrest Gump boards the school bus and meets Jenny. Describing that moment, he lists the many moments in his childhood he doesn't remember. And then, in contrast to those forgotten moments, he tells us, "But I do remember the first time I heard the sweetest voice in the wide world."

"From that day on," says Forrest, his life changed. And the moment that changed it was a moment of human connection.

Surely a defining moment in the story of *Bonnie and Clyde* is the moment the bond is forged between the outlaw lovers. The same is true for the pairs in *Thelma & Louise* and *Beauty and the Beast.* Notice that in all these cases, these connections are so fundamental, so defining, that they find their way into the titles of the films.

Wrenching disconnections — betrayals, breakups, firings, desertions, deaths — can also create moments that define characters.

In the third act of Shakespeare's *Hamlet*, the romantic tie between Hamlet and Ophelia ruptures in a single moment of

---

* Claudia Hunter Johnson, *Crafting Short Screenplays That Connect*, 4th ed., Focal Press, 2015.

operatic verbal violence. The encounter unfolds when Ophelia's father forces her to meet with Hamlet to return his love letters and break off their relationship, no matter her feelings for him. Hamlet's response, amplified by his faked insanity, is brutal. He tells Ophelia that despite what she thought she knew about the depth of his feelings for her, he never loved her.

"I was the more deceived," responds Ophelia. We can hear in her words the sting of Hamlet's sudden rejection.

Hamlet famously tells Ophelia "Get thee to a nunnery" so that she doesn't become "a breeder of sinners." He follows up with a blistering string of curses and insults.

Anguished, Ophelia cries out, "O, help him, you sweet heavens!" and "Heavenly powers, restore him!"

Her prayers notwithstanding, Hamlet rejects her and leaves her.

Thinking more of her beloved than herself, Ophelia exclaims, "Oh, what a noble mind is here o'erthrown!" Only later does she give voice to her own overwhelming grief. "Oh, woe is me, T' have seen what I have seen, see what I see!"

This spectacular moment of disconnection ruins Ophelia. Not only does it sever her bond with the man she loves, it leads her to her tragic death. For the audience of this story, Ophelia's subsequent drowning, a disconnection from life itself, can only be understood in light of her defining moment of disconnection from Hamlet.

Some characters, and some relationships, are defined not by a single moment of connection or disconnection but by a tortured series of moments of bonding and separation. The epic 1939 film *Gone with the Wind* tells a story like this, one punctuated by moments of connection, missed connection, disconnection, and reconnection between Rhett Butler and Scarlett O'Hara.

Other stories drive toward a climactic moment of connection that pays off the entire preceding storyline, redefining the lives of the characters so completely that the audience can imagine the new life that follows the end of the movie. *Sleepless in Seattle* builds toward an ending like this. Meg Ryan's Annie hears the voice of Tom Hanks' Sam on the radio relatively early in the movie. She exchanges letters with his son Jonah, flies to Seattle, watches Sam from a distance, and even says hi to him from across a highway. But these are all tenuous near-connections, or near-misses. Only after Annie travels to New York City near the end of the film, and only after she breaks up with her fiancé, a significant disconnection, and only after she makes her way to the top of the Empire State Building looking for Sam, and only after she misses finding him there, does she finally meet Jonah face to face and, through Jonah, Sam.

In that quiet encounter, Sam and Annie face one another, taking in the presence of the other, an encounter so different from the noisy, frenetic, conflict-drenched expectation we might have for a movie climax.

Sam says to Annie, "We better go." When we hear those words, we fear along with Annie that he might be disconnecting from her, telling her goodbye. But then he says two more words to Annie that clarify his meaning: "Shall we?"

He reaches toward her in invitation.

We can locate the precise climax of the film in the next shot. It's a closeup of Sam's hand extended. No one speaks. No fireworks explode. We simply see Annie place her hand in Sam's. We see the circuit completed. The connection established. We feel the emotional wallop. We imagine what follows. And it's all we need.

Might it be possible for a defining moment to occupy the place where connection and disconnection collide?

The 1990 film *Awakenings*, based on the book by Oliver Sacks and adapted for the screen by Steven Zaillian, provides precisely that sort of poignant moment. It occurs at the boundary not only between before and after but between connection and disconnection.

Leonard, played by Robert De Niro, has been housed for decades in a hospital for neurologic patients. Now a middle-aged man, he lives in a kind of stupor, suffering the lingering effects of a case of encephalitis he contracted as a boy. Many other patients in the hospital are in the same condition, written off by their doctors as empty shells.

Dr. Sayer, played by Robin Williams, is a neurologist new to the hospital who discovers that these patients are far more than empty shells. They are people, locked inside their bodies, unable to communicate but alive and present. In a leap of creative pharmacology, Sayer tests a new drug on De Niro's Leonard and the other patients. They awaken.

The sudden reconnection between these patients and a world that has long since passed them by comes fraught with emotion. When they look in the mirror and reconnect with themselves, seeing for the first time how they've aged, we feel more emotion. A friendship forms between Sayer and Leonard, another emotional connection. And Leonard, who has never experienced romance, begins a tender relationship with a young woman who visits the hospital to see her father, a long-time patient.

Then the miracle drug that awakened Leonard begins to fail. The symptoms of his illness begin to reassert themselves. He slips back toward catatonia and the terrible isolation of disconnection.

Leonard describes his experience to Sayer. "I can't read anymore. The words are written too slow. I keep going back to the beginning, to the beginning, and trying . . . "

Sayer tries to reassure his friend, but there's no denying that Leonard is slipping away.

LEONARD: I'm grotesque . . . grotesque . . . grotesque . . .

He is a man consumed by illness. With a voice that is flat and limbs that are bent and hands that are twisted and a grimace that can only hint at the great depth of the despair he is suffering.

LEONARD: Look at me and tell me I am not.

It's over and Leonard knows it. And though he won't admit it, so does Sayer. Leonard barely gets the words out—

LEONARD: This . . . isn't . . . me.

Later that day, Leonard is in the cafeteria, seated opposite the young woman who has awakened his romantic interest. Both of them are painfully aware of the disconnection wrenching them apart.

He may not have looked like a patient when Paula first met him, but he does now. It's all she can do to not break down in front of him.

PAULA: . . . I worked . . . I had friends over . . . I went dancing . . . that's about it . . .

Leonard, ticcing, nods, smiles through his grimace, imagining those things.

PAULA: I know, I should do something with my life.

LEONARD: Like what? Those are great things. I've never done any of those things.

PAULA: You will.

Leonard shakes his head "no."

LEONARD: They'll never let me out of this place. They shouldn't.

They consider each other for several moments — the one young and healthy; the other, old and ill.

LEONARD: I'm not well. I feel well inside when I see you. I wish you could see what's inside. Instead of this.

PAULA: I can see it.

Silence. As much as Leonard wants to say "I love you," he knows he cannot, that it would be ludicrous. Instead:

LEONARD: Goodbye.

He holds out one of his shaking hands to her. She reaches to it, places her hand on it, holds it, and the shaking slowly, slowly, slowly begins to subside.

She lifts him gently out of his wheelchair and leads him away from the table. She arranges his arms in such a way that he is sort of holding her and begins to slowly dance with him.

Some patients glance up from their food. Servers glance up from their work. All watch with a sort of reverie the couple dancing without music. They watch as Leonard's tics gradually disappear. They watch as he finds a sense of grace and ease, as he borrows her grace and ease. They watch him become, simply, a man dancing with a woman.

From somewhere, perhaps imagined, there is music, a quiet melody played on a piano.

In this emotion-laden scene, we feel at once the agony of the disconnection and the sweetness of the connection happening, full force, in the same instant. Neither will pass this way again. It is a defining moment for both of these melancholy dancers.

A Dream or Longing Is Awakened

If, as in *Sleepless in Seattle*, a connection atop the Empire State Building can end a movie, can the awakening of a dream or longing launch one?

Screenwriter Phil Alden Robinson opens his screenplay for the 1989 film *Field of Dreams*, based on the novel by W. P. Kinsella, with a story narrated by his lead character, Ray Kinsella. Ray talks about his love of baseball. He tells about his wife talking him, a native New Yorker, into buying a farm in her native Iowa when he was thirty-eight. And then he says, "But until I heard The Voice . . . I'd never done a crazy thing in my whole life."

Hear the before-and-after language in Ray's line, the telltale sign that we've stumbled upon a defining moment.

Robinson's screenplay describes the moment when Ray is working in the cornfield and a disembodied voice whispers to him:

> THE VOICE: "If you build it, he will come."
>
> Ray looks up and around, but sees nothing that could be the source of this sound. All around him are empty fields. He stands quietly for a few moments, then goes back to work.
>
> THE VOICE: "If you build it, he will come."
>
> Ray jerks his head in all directions to see where this voice is coming from, but again, he sees nothing unusual — just the furrowed fields and a few hundred feet away, the massive old farmhouse with a sagging veranda on three sides.

Later, the mystified Ray is out in the fields again when he hears the voice say one more time, "If you build it, he will come."

The screenplay reads:

Ray shakes his head and repeats the words to himself.

RAY: If you build it . . .

As he thinks about these words, some unexplained impulse causes Ray to turn his head deliberately toward a portion of the cornfield between him and the house.

In a flash cut, Ray sees:

A BASEBALL FIELD

For the briefest of moments, the dreamlike image of a baseball field at night, illuminated by floodlights, flares over the lawn. Standing on the edge of the field is the figure of a man with his back to us. Before we can see anything else, the image disappears.

Ray's eyes widen.

RAY: . . . he will come.

Later still, Ray discusses his vision with his wife Annie.

RAY: I think I know what "If you build it, he will come" means.

ANNIE: Oooh, why do I not think this is a good thing?

RAY: I think it means if I build a baseball field out there, Shoeless Joe Jackson will get to come back and play ball again.

Ray has had an experience. As a result, a crazy notion has gripped him, one he can now put into words. A dream has awakened. This dream will drive the rest of Ray's actions in the film, threaten to bankrupt his family, create an improbable second chance for a team of discredited baseball players, and ultimately heal a brokenness that festers inside Ray.

Only those who comprehend the defining moment in which Ray's harebrained dream was born can comprehend Ray.

Ray Kinsella represents a broad group of characters who pursue a range of often eccentric dreams and longings with obsessive focus. For writers and actors — and indeed for the audience — the key to our understanding of these obsessive characters and the key to our investment in their quixotic quests often lies in our discovery of the moments that give rise to their dreams.

Healing or Growth Takes Place

Unspeakable things happen to us in this life. We suffer wounds to our bodies, to our minds, to our souls. Dreams die. Innocence is stolen. Our hearts are torn. So terrible are these wounds, we should die — but we don't. We live on, and our wounds persist. We carry our damage with us. And that creates a need for healing. Sometimes, those moments come, wonderful moments, bathed in joy that eclipses sorrow. Our characters reflect this reality.

One such character is Dia Vandy, a boy of the Mende tribe of Sierra Leone, a character written by Edward Zwick and Marshall Herskovitz in their screenplay for the 2006 action drama *Blood Diamond*. Early in the film, the fourteen-year-old boy is abducted from his home by the rebel R.U.F. army. The R.U.F. utilize machete-wielding child soldiers to mutilate and murder. These rebels drug the teenaged Dia. They force him to participate in their atrocities. They inflict such damage on his soul that it becomes difficult to believe restoration is possible.

Dia's father Solomon throws himself into a search for his lost son. To find Dia, he partners with a South African diamond merchant named Archer who believes Solomon can lead him to a large diamond Solomon has buried near an R.U.F. camp. When at last Solomon locates Dia in the rebel camp, the father is overjoyed. He approaches Dia in the dark, silently revealing himself to his son. But Dia responds to the sight of his father not with joy but suspicion, hostility, and fear.

Zwick and Herskovitz describe the psychological injury that has transformed Dia and underlies his reaction:

> Three months of horror, of depravation, of trauma, of unspeakable acts have taken root in the soul of this young boy. His face contorts in struggle. Then —
>
> DIA: GET AWAY FROM ME! GET AWAY! (screaming) FARMER! TRAITOR!

Hearing Dia's cry, rebels swarm in, and Solomon is captured. Dia has been remade into the enemy and has no wish to be rescued by his father or restored to his family.

An R.U.F. colonel, aware that Solomon has buried a large diamond nearby, forces Solomon to dig for it at gunpoint. As Solomon digs first in one spot, then another, Archer, the diamond merchant, strikes. He shoots the colonel dead and frees Solomon.

Knowing that more rebel soldiers are approaching, Solomon hurriedly locates the true spot where he hid the gem. He digs. But as Archer reloads his weapon, he notices the boy Dia standing opposite him in the clearing, holding a 9mm handgun. Dia aims the weapon at Archer with deadly purpose.

Solomon looks up from his digging, sees Dia, and speaks his son's name.

SOLOMON: Dia—

Dia's eyes flicker from Archer to Solomon and then back.

SOLOMON: Dia, look at me.

Dia looks into Solomon's eyes.

SOLOMON: You are Dia Vandy. Of the proud Mende. Your mother loves you—and she waits by the fire making plantains and red palm stew with your sister, N'yanda, and the new baby.

Solomon moves closer to his son, who has redirected the gun toward his father.

SOLOMON: The cows wait for you. And Babu the wild dog who minds no one but you.

Solomon moves even closer to the armed boy as tears well in the eyes of father and son.

SOLOMON: And I am your father who loves you. And you will go home with me, and be my son.

He walks right up to him, ignoring the gun, and wraps his arms around him.

Dia goes limp, the gun hangs loosely at his side—as he allows himself to be held.

In this deeply emotional moment, Dia experiences a first small step of healing on what will no doubt be a long and difficult road to restoration. But this moment is the pivot point, the one that forms the line between before and after. It is a moment that will define Dia, his relationship with himself, with the R.U.F., with his father, with his family, and with his future. Understanding not only the moment of injury but also this subsequent moment of healing becomes key to understanding Dia Vandy.

* * *

Moments of before and after. Moments of injury, of loss, of emotional or spiritual transformation, of birth, of death, of growth, of decision, of discovery, of learning, of connection, of disconnection, of a dream awakening, of healing. Some defining moments share just one or two of these characteristics. Others share many. In every case, if we understand these qualities that characterize defining moments, we begin to recognize them when we see them in literature or on the stage or screen. We begin to notice them in our own lives. And we become ready to craft them or discover them in the characters we write, direct, and portray.

* * *

This isn't a book for the armchair observer. It doesn't intend only to make you know more. It aims to equip you with a new ability. To that end, you will find exercises throughout the remaining chapters. As with a gym membership card, you experience the value of these exercises when you put them to use. To the extent that you exert yourself with these challenges, your ability will grow. Your characters will deepen. The grip and hold of your stories will gather strength.

To sharpen your ability to recognize defining moments when you see them in the work of others:

1. Pick a film or series with which you have connected.
2. Rewatch the film or the series pilot.
3. Look for the moments that define the most memorable and relatable characters.

4. Write a short paragraph describing each moment you identify.
5. Make a note of the characteristics listed in this chapter that ring true for each moment.

As you gain awareness of defining moments in the film and TV you watch, you prepare yourself to do the creative work that lies ahead.

3.
Discovering Your Own Defining Moments

EDVARD MUNCH, THE NORWEGIAN ARTIST WHO CREATED THE UNIVERSALLY recognized painting *The Scream*, once said, "I do not believe in the art which is not the compulsive result of humanity's urge to open its heart."

Kathy thought along the same lines as Munch. When she began to teach developing writers about defining moments, she took Coleman Luck's insight and pushed it a step further. She made it personal. After explaining what Luck had taught us years earlier about defining moments, she told students, "Before you can tell someone else's story, you have to understand your own."

That seems to make sense. For though we actors and writers and directors create characters, we don't create them out of nothing. The something from which we create characters, more often than not, is ourselves. When it comes to understanding what makes a person tick, we must draw on our own experience of being a person. Like no one else, we have access to our own invisible inner lives. We feel our own fears. We soar on our own triumphs. We suffer our own agonies. We love our own loves. As we engage in the project of understanding characters, we are our own richest resource. Isn't this Constantin Stanislavski's foundational insight in his seminal *An Actor Prepares*?

And so, again, "Before you can tell someone else's story, you have to understand your own."

If only that were a simple project.

If only each of us could take five minutes, jot down the list of the half-dozen moments that have formed the person we are today, provide a neat story capturing the drama of each moment, and then go on to invest our insights into creating unforgettable characters.

It turns out it's harder than that. Some of our stories mortify us. Others buoy us with wide-eyed gratitude for the wonder of being alive in this world. Others we can only recall with anguish. And some are so traumatizing or made their mark on us so early that our conscious mind doesn't know them. We only see the scars or recognize that we've always walked with a limp.

Kathy quotes a favorite author, Frederick Buechner, in this regard. Buechner, an American writer and theologian, was writing with advice to his fellow preachers but could just as well have been advising any one of us in the storytelling profession. "Preachers," Buechner wrote, "must address themselves to the fullness of who we are and to the emptiness too, the emptiness where grace and peace belong but mostly are not, because terrible and wonderful things have happened to us all."

Things so terrible and wonderful, some of them, that they've changed us permanently. Sometimes we've changed for the better, sometimes for the worse. And digging back through our own histories in search of those terrible and wonderful things can bring us to a realization of the fullness of who we are. It can make us feel, perhaps for the first time, like we're full members of the human race.

Artist Vincent van Gogh, in a letter to his youngest sister, spoke of the link between artist and artwork, actor and performance, book and author. "You read books to borrow therefrom the force to stimulate your activity," he wrote, "but I read books searching for the man who has written them." Van Gogh understood art as a means of self-discovery accompanied by self-revelation.

We may feel this sort of personal discovery and disclosure isn't necessary. We can do good character work without dredging up our pasts. We may feel it isn't prudent. Why dwell on often painful memories? Or we may fear that this degree of self-awareness isn't safe. What might happen to us if we open the door to the sometimes unspeakable events of our childhoods, to our personal tragedies, to our unrealized dreams? And what right have we to parade our personal triumphs, our loving and fulfilling connections, our dreams come true?

Recently, a young storyteller told Chris he had a true story to tell but needed to tell it privately. It was something he described as "monumental" in his life but also something he said he wasn't ready to talk about in a public setting.

His feeling wasn't wrong. We're not ready to share every experience we've ever had. And we certainly don't yet *understand* every experience we've had. Storytellers do well to consider both the audience and the timing of their storytelling. In the course of our lives, we've heard stories that we will never tell, not simply because doing so would break a confidence but because the story itself is so intensely personal, painful, vivid, intimate, and raw that it overwhelms the listener like a kind of emotional pornography.

And yet the challenge remains: "Before you can tell someone else's story, you have to understand your own."

If the core idea behind character-defining moments rings true — that much of a character's formation owes to a relatively small number of defining events or experiences — that's because it's true not just of characters. It's true of living people. It's true of *us*. And a writer or actor's ability to craft credible, relatable characters begins with the insight, vulnerability, and honesty that accompanies the excavation of our own defining moments.

Tony Hale speaks of recognizing both the emotional costs and the payoffs for actors tapping into their own defining moments. "Many times, the reason I don't want to do that is out of insecurity. Or it's out of fear. For many years, I would say I kind of just played that idea of a character, or I went through the motions. Because the stuff in my life, I don't necessarily want to go back to it. I don't want to go back to the bullying in middle school. I don't want to go back to the family trauma. I don't have a desire to go back to that. So when I would read these characters and I would know they went through this, I think I played an idea just out of protection. Rather than being, like, okay, I can tap into this. I can daydream about this a little bit. I'll still be okay. When I allowed myself to do that, I think it took me to a more vulnerable place with the character. That's where the risk comes in. I did a play recently in San Francisco. Terrifying experience. I really allowed myself to dive in, and it was a beautiful experience. But the process was really challenging."

When auditioning for a role, Hale says he's found value in tapping into the humanity he finds within himself to distinguish his performance. "Whenever I tried to play an idea of a character, there's a thousand other guys who can play that idea much better than I ever could. But if I find those traits within myself and resonate with it and bring that to the table, nobody else can do that. And not only can nobody else do that, that's going to bring out the most authentic performance in me. If I take those characteristics in myself, that's going to give the most authentic audition. I might not get the role, but no one will have put that out like I did."

We long ago accepted the challenge of working to discover our own defining moments. It's a project that has stretched over years and remains far from complete. We'll recount some of those moments here in an effort to model the work we advise our fellow storytellers to undertake, to illustrate what these moments can look like in the lives of actual people, and to guide you into a series of practical exercises that can help you unearth the sometimes hidden, often emotion-laden, wonderful and terrible moments that shape you.

Kathy's father grew up in a blue-collar town in western Pennsylvania, the son of a schoolteacher and a self-taught engineer for Pittsburgh Plate Glass. He was born during the Great Depression and grew up during World War II. He married a local girl he met at a dance, flunked out of Penn State's mechanical engineering program, got drafted into the army and posted to Iceland. After the army, with three children — Kathy was the middle child — and a mortgage on a tiny house in Hyde Park, PA, he worked his way back into the Penn State engineering program. He moved his whole family back to State College, where Kathy attended kindergarten while he earned his degree. For all the years of Kathy's growing up, he supported his family. He was faithful to his wife. He sang in the church choir. He volunteered for the Boy Scouts.

Kathy can't remember that he ever told her that he loved her.

When he died in his eighty-seventh year, Kathy wrote words she read at his funeral. She sought to honor all that was sterling about him while acknowledging his broken humanity. Taking inspiration from the poem "Where I'm From" by George Ella Lyon, she wrote in her father's voice, giving words to a man who too infrequently used his. Snatches of Kathy's eulogy capture her experience of her dad:

I am from silence and music ...
A child of promise in a time of war ...
A boy who dreams but becomes a man ...
I am from quiet and commitment and words never said.

From her perspective as an adult, Kathy could see her father as a boy shaped by depression and world war. She could honor his quiet commitment to her and her family. But she could also acknowledge with honesty the words she needed to hear but didn't because they were never said.

She arrived at her early adolescence without the sense of worth a father's simple expression of love can invest in his daughter.

And then her parents took her to Ohio to attend a relative's wedding when she was twelve or thirteen years old. She sat in the pew beside her Uncle Carl. He was the young uncle, the charming, handsome one married to her father's youngest sister, Kay. Kathy was happy to find herself sitting beside Carl and his pretty wife, both of them dressed up and looking glamorous and almost like movie stars. In the moments before the ceremony began, Carl looked around the church. Then he looked at Kay, all dolled up on his right, and at Kathy, in her prettiest dress on his left, and this handsome, charming man said, "I'm sitting here between the two most beautiful women in the room."

Those words set Kathy's heart soaring even as they made an indelible mark on her, igniting a new dream. For the first time, she imagined finding a man who would talk to her like that, who would put his feelings for her into words, and who would speak those words out loud. She began to dream of a man who would cherish her.

Before her experience at the wedding, Kathy didn't harbor that dream. After the wedding, her dream informed her decisions about whom to imagine and later to date. It guided her choices about which relationships to avoid or end. It played a key role in whom she chose to marry. The change that took place invisibly in a twelve-year-old's heart proved permanent and defining.

Chris can count on his fingers the movies he watched growing up: *Peter Pan. The Wizard of Oz. Willy Wonka and the Chocolate Factory. Chitty Chitty Bang Bang. True Grit.* When he watched television, he took in reruns of *Gilligan's Island, Leave It to Beaver,* and *Green Acres.* None of it stirred his soul. In high school, he excelled at math and physics. He wrote some poems. He drew stick figures and shot two or three Super 8 movies, the least awful of which he titled "A Bloody Day in the Old West." He wrote comedy sketches, mostly mock news broadcasts cobbled together from material plagiarized from *Reader's Digest.* As part of a group called Harmony in Our Hands, he performed musical numbers in sign language for deaf children. He started a radio station playing recordings of The Jackson 5 over his battery-powered CB radio. He couldn't imagine a career that could encompass all of his interests and that wouldn't bore him silly. He was a socially awkward boy who spent hours building miniatures for an elaborate model railroad layout in his basement and shooting stop-motion movies alone. He longed for human connection but didn't know how to make friends. He couldn't figure out what kept him locked in isolation. Everyone around him seemed happier and more blessed with friends than he. As he imagined his future, he feared he would grow old alone, a condition that even in his teen years he found as excruciating as a knife wound that refused to heal.

But one day while he was a college student, lightning struck. He saw the 1980 film *Ordinary People* and experienced two life-changing revelations.

The film tells the story of a high school student played by

Timothy Hutton who is just returning home from three months in a psychiatric hospital after attempting suicide. He goes back to his school, sings in the choir, and looks like he's fine. Like he's got his act together. He looks like everyone who surrounded Chris in high school — attractive, smiling, popular people who Chris thought were leading relatively perfect and painless lives. But *Ordinary People*'s writer, director, and actors let their audience in on a secret. Unbeknownst to anyone in his life, Hutton's character is enduring enormous, life-threatening emotional pain. His mother, searingly portrayed by Mary Tyler Moore, is blind to his suffering. She is in fact compounding it by her own resentment and self-absorption. Chris remembers sitting in the theater on the edge of his seat, terrified that at any moment this great kid is going to kill himself and nobody around him knows to be worried.

That was Chris's first revelation. For the first time in his life, he saw that people who appeared well put together and superficially happy could be suffering great pain — in fact, could be at the point of self-destruction. He learned that he wasn't the only one pretending to be happier than he was. This revelation transformed the way he saw people. On his best days, it even elevated the way he treated people.

And this brought Chris to his second life-changing revelation. For the first time, he saw the power of film to provoke radical new insights, and he found himself irresistibly attracted to the possibility of wielding this sight-giving power of film.

Decades later, these twin revelations — that people are often suffering and must be treated with compassion, and that film has the power to give sight to the blind — remain two of Chris's core beliefs. These beliefs derive not from any life experience but from revelations, epiphanies, he experienced while a filmmaker told a story on the screen. This experience of epiphany is what drew Chris to his lifelong pursuit of a career as a storyteller in Hollywood. It is what drives him to continue writing for the screen in spite of all the difficulties presented by that pursuit.

Chris's experience watching *Ordinary People* redefined him. It created a boundary of before and after. He made a life-changing discovery. He learned a profound lesson. And a dream was awakened. Knowing about this defining moment in his life provides significant insight into who he is and why he does what he does. It defines him to this day.

* * *

Now we come to your moment of action. Here you turn the spotlight on yourself to explore, discover, and examine your own stories.

Which moments define you?

To find them, you may need to dig in ground you've treated as off limits. It's likely that some of the moments that define you have already sprung to your mind. Others may take persistent digging in soil that will resist yielding its treasures. This process will require you to think and feel deeply, to search the hidden places of your heart for memories, some of them hilarious, others excruciating, others joyous, some terrifying. You may do more than squirm. Many of the emotions associated with defining moments are uncomfortable. Some are close to unbearable. Others send us soaring. We invite you to push through the emotion to explore the moments that have defined you so that your discoveries can inform the characters you create and play.

An important caveat: While artists must risk discomfort, some of us have lived through events so traumatizing that touching them can cause more than pain. It may cause further damage. We caution you to pay attention to your response as you approach moments that have damaged you, especially if you sense that you may be taking on fresh damage. In some cases, we need to allow more time to pass or for more healing to occur before we're ready to unearth our worst moments. And in some cases, we do well to approach these moments with the support and care of a mental health professional. Remember that this work is about you understanding your own story so that you can tell somebody else's. No character exists that is worth more than you and your emotional well-being.

Locating the Moment a Dream or Longing Awoke in You

Let's begin by looking for the moment you began pining for something you don't yet have but which you've long desired.

- You may dream of a career — or a bigger, more successful career than you have at the moment — as an actor, a writer, a director, an editor, a novelist, or a producer.
- You may harbor dreams of the day you can quit your job or escape from the city to the country or from the country to the city.
- You may yearn to travel to Bali or Paris or Machu Picchu or Iowa.
- You could be saving your nickels to buy a sailboat, an RV, dental work, or a hot tub.
- You might want your team to win the Stanley Cup or the NBA Finals.
- You may dream of going back to school.
- You could simply want to find love that lasts.
- You may long for a child.
- You might dream of living long enough to see your son's wedding or your daughter released from prison.

- You might dream of turning the tide against racial injustice, child abuse, extreme poverty, or climate change.
- You could be living for the day your doctor tells you after eighteen months of treatment that you're free of cancer.

If your abiding desire wasn't already at the top of your mind, reading that list might have triggered a realization about what you long for. Some of us know exactly what we want. We carry it like a banner. Others struggle to find it, perhaps not believing that we deserve anything good or doubting that it's right to want something for ourselves. Some feel embarrassed or ashamed to admit the thing we want, even to ourselves. Ruminate on the question until the thing you desire comes into focus.

Whatever it is, name it, then write it down. Using words, pin your prize to the page.

Now ask yourself, where did that dream come from? When was it born? If your longing is a house ablaze, when was the match struck?

If you can locate the moment your dream or longing awakened, use your imagination to step inside the scene and look around. Where are you? Who is present? What's happening? Where does the scene begin? Where does it end? What does it feel like? What is the lasting change this moment makes in your life?

Your answers to the questions above become the raw material out of which you can write down the story of your defining moment in a paragraph, like a scene. A paragraph of two to four sentences is often the right size. Not so short that it fails to capture what happened; not so long that it loses focus.

Choose a place to save this paragraph. Treat it as precious. It's the record of a moment that defines you. It will also serve as a touchstone for the creative character work that lies ahead.

Locating the Moment You Suffered a Lasting Wound or a Grievous Loss

The clown fish Nemo, namesake of *Finding Nemo*, has a broken flipper. Dory, Marlin's sidekick in *Finding Nemo* and star of the sequel, *Finding Dory*, suffers short-term memory loss. Captain Hook has his hook, Tiny Tim his crutch, the patriarch Jacob his limp. Frodo Baggins aches from the stab wound he received on Weathertop. George Bailey of *It's a Wonderful Life* has his bad ear. Forrest has his leg braces and, as he will agree, may not be a smart man. Michael Corleone carries the eventual death of his father and the murder of his young Italian wife. J.M. Barrie bears the weight of not only his own grief over the loss of his brother but also his mother's grief. In *Saving Private Ryan*, the first thing Spielberg reveals about Tom Hanks' Captain Miller, as his army landing craft approaches Omaha Beach, is his hand tremor. At the beginning of *Titanic*, Rose is so tortured she's ready to fling herself into the North Atlantic.

Many of our best-loved stories feature broken characters. These characters are flawed like us. We identify with them as they struggle, imperfect, hobbling toward their goal, sometimes succumbing, sometimes overcoming. Because that's how some of us live our days and fight our battles. With one broken arm tied behind our backs.

If we, like our characters, are wounded, flawed, or broken, we should ask, "When and how did I receive this damage?" Sometimes, we know. We remember every detail of the battle on Weathertop. Other times we have to make inquiries, unlayering ourselves in our archeological dig into ourselves. Sometimes, as we expose deeper layers of soil and rock, we discover the answer that has lain buried — perhaps fiercely guarded — for long ages. The discovery may give us important insight into ourselves. It may even turn us toward healing.

In the years after our son Peter completed treatment for his brain tumor, the cancer didn't return. We celebrated his sixth birthday, his seventh and eighth. But the treatment that saved his life exacted a price. The surgery that cut out the malignant tumor also impaired his balance and coordination so drastically that he needed seven months of physical therapy to learn to walk again. Even after years of recovery, his attempts at riding a bicycle never got beyond a harrowing, weaving clown-wobble, his wayward left foot repeatedly slipping off the pedal, us racing alongside to catch him when he inevitably toppled. The radiation beamed at his developing brain and the chemotherapy dripped into his veins caused further damage even as it worked to heal him of the cancer. His hearing was damaged. His eyes stopped tracking together. His growth slowed. His thyroid failed. And over time, a widening intellectual gap opened between Peter and his peers.

Kathy felt profound gratitude that Peter had survived when many other children diagnosed with brain cancer do not. Still, some afternoons she would drive past a high school football practice and pull her car to the curb, watching the players run through their drills, strong and tall, galloping like gazelles, knocking one another flat and bouncing back to their feet. On those afternoons, she ached.

What was wrong with her? she wondered. Why couldn't she let go of the sadness and feel only joy that Peter continued to live?

She tried to raise these questions with Chris. She told him about her stops outside high school football fields. She asked, "Do you sometimes let yourself wonder who Peter would have been?" and "Don't you ever imagine?"

When Kathy talked like this, Chris felt himself exploding out of his skin with a discomfort he couldn't bear or explain. He wasn't capable of engaging in the conversation Kathy invited. He feared it would kill him. So Kathy bore her agonized and confusing feelings alone.

As years passed and it became clear that no amount of extra effort, therapy, or time would allow Peter to make up the ground he'd lost or close the gap between the life his parents had dreamed for him and the one he actually got, Kathy began meeting with other families whose children had been diagnosed with brain tumors. Along with her friend Gianna McMillan, a dynamo mom whose son Ben had a brain tumor history similar to Peter's, she founded an organization to bring these families together to share their stories and learn from one another. At one of these gatherings, parents of surviving children mingled with parents whose children had died. Kathy listened as one of these bereaved mothers spoke of her grief over the loss of her child. The pain she described dwarfed Kathy's. But before Kathy could lapse into renewed feelings of guilt that she allowed herself to feel any sadness at all, this mother spoke to her. This wise and generous mother said that as she listened to the stories of the parents whose children had lived, she realized something she hadn't seen before.

"You've lost something, too."

They'd lost dreams and futures. Their children's carefree childhoods. And for some of these survivors, they'd lost the prospect of driver's licenses and proms and college admissions and weddings and children of their own.

"But," this mother said, "no one has given you permission to grieve." She spoke with the authority only a bereaved parent possessed. "I give you permission."

Something in Kathy broke open. Her loss had been dragged into the light from the shadows in which it had hidden unnamed. It had been acknowledged and named.

"You've lost something, too."

The moment when we said goodbye to Peter as nurses wheeled him into surgery to remove the malignancy from his brain had been the last moment we'd looked at him while he was still whole. It was a moment from which he never fully returned. It was a moment necessary to save his life. But it was simultaneously a moment of terrible loss.

We've learned over the years that it isn't useful to compare one person's losses to another's. Every heart knows its own pain, the ancient wisdom literature tells us. Pain is not erased just because someone else suffers more, as someone always does.

What about you? What loss have you suffered that pains and impoverishes you to this day? What wound have you received that has left a permanent limp or scar? Sometimes these moments hide behind undeserved shame, resisting our efforts to examine them. Other times they bury themselves in legitimate guilt, requiring that we face up to our own responsibility for ways we've failed ourselves. Looking at these moments will require courage. And it may warrant the help of someone who you know cares about you. In some cases, you may benefit from the guidance of a counselor or therapist.

If you can locate the moment you suffered that loss or received that wound, dare to use your imagination to step inside the scene. As you did when you examined the moment a dream or desire awakened, look around that scene. Where are you? Who is present? What's happening? Where does the scene begin? Where does it end? What does it feel like? What is the lasting change this moment makes in your life?

Collect the answers to these questions as the raw material out of which you can write down the story of your defining moment in a paragraph. Write two to four sentences capturing the scene.

Save this paragraph along with the descriptions of your other defining moments. Together, they form a multidimensional portrait of you and the experiences that shape you. And they equip you to build multidimensional characters in your work as a storyteller.

Locating a Moment You Began to Heal

If the moment of Peter's brain tumor diagnosis and treatment represents a moment of loss for Kathy, the moment she received a bereaved mother's permission to grieve became the moment her heart turned toward healing. That encounter became a pivot point. That mother's words became a balm. They didn't restore Peter's balance or thyroid or intellect. They didn't wipe away Kathy's pain. But before that moment, her sadness over Peter's losses felt ingrown, confusing, and illicit. Afterward, it felt honest and legitimate. It was permitted. Kathy could finally allow herself to grieve Peter's losses. She could grieve her own. And she could begin to tread onto fresh emotional ground, holding her sadness and pain in one hand while at the same instant holding her gratitude and joy in the other. She could inhabit her life's bittersweet reality in a way that allowed her to embrace the bitter and the sweet.

For Kathy, this experience created a new boundary that separated before from after. A deep and lasting emotional change took place. Linked inextricably to her moment of loss, this moment became for her a moment of healing. It's a moment that continues to shape her inner life to this day.

It's in the nature of healing, like the growth of children and oak trees, that it often takes place over time. Mostly, healing creeps up on us. The extended process often begins, however, in a moment.

Have you experienced such a moment when healing began? In contrast to the sharp and often dramatic moments of injury that come with pain and demand our attention, moments of healing can arrive with a whisper. They can escape our notice. You may need to reflect on your past injuries to realize that, in fact, you no longer walk with that limp. You no longer guard that wound. You have by some amazing and undetected process gotten better. When did that healing process begin? What was the turning point? Can you locate a moment like that in your experience?

If you can, place yourself within the moment when you turned toward healing. It could be the moment you found the therapist who made a difference, or the session when you finally spoke out loud the thing that had been done to you. It could be the moment you admitted you were an addict. Or a moment when brave friends intervened to call you back to yourself. Look around the scene. Who is with you? What words are spoken? How does it feel? When do you know something has changed?

Write a paragraph describing this moment. Save it with the records of your other defining moments. Draw on it when you build characters to undergird moments of healing that will resonate with authenticity because they're based on the truth of your own experience.

Locating a Moment You Made a Life-Changing Choice, Discovery, or Commitment

Moments of discovery and decision can set our course in dramatic and enduring ways. We enlist in the Marines. We get engaged. We discover the lump. We learn we're adopted. We discover we're attracted not to her but to him. We find out they cheated on us. We vow revenge. We learn the scan is clean. We meet our first grandchild.

Many times, decisions follow discoveries like trains follow locomotives. In *The Godfather*, Michael Corleone discovers who ordered the attempt on his father's life, and he decides to strike back. Bryan Stevenson, in *Just Mercy*, discovers a man on Georgia's death row is innocent and decides to fight for his release.

Some decisions can be easily undone and don't rise to the level of defining moments. Other decisions, like enlisting in the Marines or gunning down a crime boss and the police captain who protects him, have lasting consequences. And some decisions are difficult to undo by design. These we call vows or pledges: A young acolyte takes her vows and becomes a nun. A bride says her vows and becomes a wife. An immigrant pledges allegiance and becomes a citizen. Government officials take oaths and become senators, representatives, justices, and presidents. In the aftermath of the tragic opening scene of *Finding Nemo*, Marlin the clown fish vows, "I'll never let anything happen to you, Nemo."

Despite the strength of our pledges, vows, and oaths, we sometimes undo them. We break vows. We violate oaths. These moments of unvowing can also rise to the level of defining moments, shaping us and our lives for years to come.

When have you made a discovery that changed your life? Or made a decision with lifelong consequences? Or made a commitment of such seriousness that it rose to the level of an oath, pledge, or vow? Or broken a vow?

Imagine yourself in that moment. What was your life before that moment? What did you feel at the precise moment of discovery, decision, commitment, or revocation of a pledge? How did you change after that moment? How does that moment shape your life to this day?

Write a paragraph that does justice to your defining moment, describing it like a scene or story. Add it to your growing collection and draw on it when you build your characters, who will make life-changing discoveries, decisions, and commitments of their own.

Locating a Moment You Experienced a Birth or Death

In an early episode of the Netflix series *The Crown*, newlywed Princess Elizabeth and her husband Prince Philip are happily touring Africa when they receive news that Elizabeth's father, King George VI, has died. In that jarring moment, Elizabeth is transformed from princess to queen. The death of her father redefines her.

We observe the same wrenching transformation in a photograph of Lyndon B. Johnson aboard Air Force One on a flight from Dallas back to Washington, D.C., the body of John F. Kennedy in the cargo hold, Johnson raising his hand to take the oath of office and become President of the United States. The death of a president redefined the life of his vice president.

Moments of birth, sometimes literal birth, sometimes metaphorical birth, can also define lives. Germany invades Poland, giving birth to Word War II. The U.S. gives violent birth to the atomic age in the bombing of Hiroshima. The introduction of the Salk vaccine in 1955 gives birth to generations who won't know the fear of polio. In 1963, the birth of Ming Ming, history's first giant panda born in captivity after years of failed attempts, staves off the otherwise imminent extinction of a species. The birth of a longed-for child after years of infertility upends a home and reverberates down the years with joy.

Moments of literal birth and death frequently declare themselves far more publicly — with birth announcements and showers, newspaper obituaries and funerals — than do moments of wounding, healing, or profound emotional or moral change. But as you examine your own history for births or deaths that have shaped you, remember that you're looking for an event that made a lasting difference in your life, one that creates in your personal formation a moment of before and after. Every person's birth and every person's death represents a noteworthy event. Not every birth and death represents a defining moment *for you*. And it's possible that the birth or death that has shaped you most may not be the birth or death of a person but of an idea, an organization, a movement, a relationship. It may hide itself from ready notice. You may need to reflect, considering several possibilities, before you recognize the birth or death that most lastingly defines you.

Once you find it, write about it. Write about what you were like before this moment, and write about who you came to be as a consequence of this moment. Add this story to your growing collection.

Locating a Moment You Experienced a Moral or Spiritual Change

When in *The Godfather* Michael Corleone chooses to embrace violence and gun down his father's enemies, more changes than his standing before the law. Something at the level of his soul shifts. When he commits murder, *he becomes a murderer.* His violent act marks him as permanently as the sculptor's blow marks the granite block.

German industrialist Oskar Schindler, in *Schindler's List*, chooses to abandon his quest to amass wealth for himself from the labor of enslaved Jews during the Nazi Holocaust and to use his position instead to protect as many as he can from deportation to Auschwitz. That decision costs Schindler everything and saves more than one thousand lives. It also reshapes the soul of a Nazi businessman so completely that he is honored by Israel's Yad Vashem in 1993 as one of the "Righteous Among the Nations." This is a moral title that acknowledges an astonishing moral reversal.

What does a moment look like that alters us *spiritually*? We can look to the 2007 horror film *I Am Legend* starring Will Smith as Dr. Robert Neville, a military virologist stationed in New York City during a global viral pandemic. With vanishingly rare exceptions, the virus kills those it infects or reduces them to zombie-like predators who hunt humanity's survivors. Over time, Neville becomes the last living human in the city, perhaps the world. Neville has seen his wife and daughter die. He's seen New York emptied. He's seen no evidence that people have survived anywhere. And this experience has crushed him. Nonetheless, he stays at his post, working in his basement lab for a cure, insisting with a kind of sad mania that he can still fix this. Every day he broadcasts a radio call into the silence of the apocalypse, hoping to connect with another survivor. No answer ever comes. Until one day, during the worst of an attack by a hive of "Darkseekers," essentially zombies, that looks like it will end Neville, Anna, a Brazilian woman played by Alice Braga, appears and rescues him.

Anna tells him she's heard of a colony of survivors somewhere in Vermont. That's where she and Ethan, the young boy who travels with her, were headed when they heard Neville's radio call.

In the screenplay, written by Mark Protosevich and Akiva Goldsman, based on the screenplay by John William & Joyce H. Corrington, based on the novel by Richard Matheson, Neville reacts violently to Anna's hope. "There's no survivors' colony," he tells her. "There's no safe zone. Nothing worked the way it was supposed to."

But Anna persists in hope. "In the mountains. There's a whole colony of people there who didn't get sick. The virus couldn't survive the cold. There's a colony . . . "

Neville explodes. "Shut up! Shut up! Everybody's dead. Everybody is dead."

Later, in a quiet moment after Neville regains his composure, Anna finds a photo of Neville's daughter. Neville tells her the girl's name was Marley, after the singer Bob Marley. To Neville's astonishment, Anna doesn't know the iconic reggae artist.

To correct this travesty, Neville tells her a story of the singer. "He had this idea, it was kind of a virologist's idea. He believed that you could cure racism and hate. Literally cure it . . . by injecting music and love into people's lives. One day he was scheduled to perform at a peace rally. Gunmen came to his house and shot him down. Two days later . . . he walked out on that stage and sang. Somebody asked him why. He said, 'The people who are trying to make this world worse are not taking a day off. How can I?' Light up the darkness."

Anna hears the echo of a hope this man Neville once nurtured. "Come with us," she says.

NEVILLE: There's no colony, Anna.

ANNA: I know, okay?

NEVILLE: How do you know, Anna? How could you know?

ANNA: God told me.

NEVILLE: God told you?

ANNA: Yes.

NEVILLE: The God.

ANNA: I know how this sounds. But something told me to turn on the radio. Something told me to come here.

NEVILLE: My voice on the radio told you to come here, Anna.

ANNA: I got here just in time to save your life. That's a

coincidence?

NEVILLE: Just stop it. Stop it. Stop.

ANNA: Neville, the world is quieter now. You just have to listen. If we listen, we can hear God's plan.

NEVILLE: God's plan? Let me tell you about your God's plan. There were six billion people on Earth when the infection hit. KV had a 90 percent kill rate. That's 5.4 billion people dead. Crashed and bled out, dead. Less than one percent immunity. That left 12 million healthy people like you, me and Ethan. The other 588 million turned into your Darkseekers. And then they got hungry. And they killed and fed on everybody. Everybody! Every single person that you or I has ever known . . . is dead! Dead! There is no God. There is no God.

Soon after this brutal exchange, Neville's home is overrun by a swarm of Darkseekers. Neville leads Anna and Ethan to his basement lab for shelter. And as the Darkseekers break down the lab door, Neville discovers that his latest experiment has reversed the effects of the virus on one of the Darkseekers he's captured to use as an experimental subject. She's recovering. The treatment works.

Seeing that the Darkseekers will overrun the lab any second, Neville experiences what we might call a spiritual epiphany, a defining moment that allows him to see beyond the dire circumstances to a kind of transcendent hope. It's a moment that invites him to rethink his despair. He sees a pattern and a plan. He's found the cure, and Anna is here to carry it to those who need it. He makes a decision and swiftly draws a vial of the recovering test subject's blood.

ANNA: Robert, what are you doing?

NEVILLE: The cure is in her blood.

He rushes Anna and Ethan through the metal hatch in the back of the lab.

NEVILLE: Go.

When Anna realizes Neville isn't coming, she says, "Come on, get in."

NEVILLE: Anna.

He places the syringe in her hand, wrapping her fingers around it.

NEVILLE: I think this is why you're here.

He begins to pull away from Anna, the onslaught of Darkseekers almost upon them.

ANNA: What are you doing?

NEVILLE: I'm listening.

ANNA: Neville, there's room. Come!

NEVILLE: They're not gonna stop. They're not gonna stop.

As he closes the hatch on them, he says, "Stay in till dawn."

Then he arms himself with a grenade and rushes the swarming Darkseekers, meeting them in a devastating fireball.

Following the explosion, we find ourselves in Vermont with Anna and Ethan, driving up to the fortified gate of a mountain compound. The gate opens, and the survivors inside welcome the new arrivals and their life-giving vial of blood.

> ANNA (V.O.): In 2009, a deadly virus burned through our civilization, pushing humankind to the edge of extinction. Dr. Robert Neville dedicated his life to the discovery of a cure and the restoration of humanity. On September 9th, 2012, at approximately 8:49 pm, he discovered that cure. And at 8:52, he gave his life to defend it. We are his legacy. This is his legend. Light up the darkness."

In this defining moment for Robert Neville, he makes a choice to step across a spiritual boundary of before and after. This moment of spiritual change redefines him, brings him back from despair, reignites his hope and his inner fight, and leads to the reshaping of the world.

When have you made a choice with lasting implications for your soul? Some of these choices may appear small and insignificant. But ancient wisdom literature tells us that the one who is faithful in small things will be faithful in large things, and the one who is unfaithful in small things will be unfaithful in large things. Dare we examine those small moments of decision and their unforeseen and often unintended fallout for our souls? What insight could we gain about our own inner lives from such an unblinking examination? And what depth could that insight enable us to lend to the characters we form?

Search for a moment when you experienced a moral or spiritual change — for better or for worse. Set aside the pride or false modesty or shame the memory may evoke so that you can stare your moment in the eye. What was the condition of your soul before that moment? What forces or motives shaped your choice? How did it feel to have made the decision you made? What did your choice lead to in the short term? What did it lead to over time?

Now write about the moment. Describe it as a short, dramatic scene. Safeguard it in the vault that holds the record of your other defining moments. Let the insights you gain from your examination of that moment inform the formation of your characters, who will sometimes live as shining saints, sometimes as depraved sinners, but will live most often somewhere on the morally ambiguous middle ground where actual humans are found.

When We Can See the Change but Can't Locate the Moment

"My account of myself is partial, haunted by that for which I can devise no definitive story," writes Judith Butler in her book *Giving an Account of Oneself.** "I cannot explain exactly why I have emerged in this way, and my efforts at narrative reconstruction are always undergoing revision. There is that in me and of me for which I can give no account."

It's possible to possess a scar but not the memory of how we received it. We might follow a lifelong dream without any recollection of how and when it awakened. Some of us carry programming that seems coded into our firmware from primordial time, imperatives and compulsions that seem to exist independent of any identifiable cause. How are we to understand a character — indeed, how are we to understand ourselves — if we can't put our finger on a defining moment that explains forces like these? We see the damage, we experience the incapacity, but we can't locate the moment we received the wound. What if we can't remember?

Is it possible that insight into the existence of a defining moment, even if we can't recall it, can help us make sense of ourselves and begin to undo some of its power and perhaps heal some of its damage?

Chris lives with a moment like that.

By the time he'd lived into his forties, Chris had enough

---

* Judith Butler, *Giving an Account of Oneself,* Fordham University Press, 2005.

self-knowledge to realize he possessed a fair number of quirks. The prospect of looming confrontation ate at him like drain cleaner in his lower bowel. Actual confrontation exhausted him. When he carried a book onto an airplane, he irrationally hid its cover from the eyes of nearby passengers. When he suffered disappointments, he couldn't admit them to himself, let alone anyone else, so he tap-danced with the manic energy of a dervish to explain that they weren't really disappointments at all. He hated making mistakes; being found at fault for the smallest of things felt to him like an existential threat, dangerous as a firing squad. He hated making phone calls or asking friends for help. He avoided friendships with men, feeling safer with women. He remembers suffering embarrassment about his body as early as first grade, when he desperately didn't want to be seen in his swimming trunks. He hid in a multitude of ways, both metaphorical and literal. He lived as if his firmest belief was that if anyone knew the truth about him, they would cease to love him.

One Fourth of July afternoon when he was twelve years old, he was in his neighbor Pam's front yard, lighting Black Cats and letting them explode in the street. Pam's older sister ran from the house. She was frantic.

"Dad's drowning in the pool in the backyard!" she shrieked. She said something about running to get her pastor and rushed down the street.

Pam, who was eleven, said, "Shit!" and ran through the open garage door into the house, presumably on her way toward the pool.

Chris didn't follow. Her didn't run toward the danger. He didn't help his friend. He didn't try to save his dying neighbor. He just put down the firecrackers and matches, turned, and walked quietly back to his house. His mother was home. He didn't speak a word to her about the tragedy unfolding next door.

When the sound of sirens approached and a fire engine stopped in front of the neighbors' house, Chris's mom covered her mouth with her hand and said, "Oh no. I hope one of the kids didn't fall in the pool."

Chris said, "They didn't," flat and emotionless, like a "bad seed" kid from a 1950s horror film.

He walked outside with his mother and watched when paramedics wheeled the lifeless body of Pam's father down the driveway. He heard his mother ask a firefighter what had happened. He heard the jaded firefighter respond, "Too much time in the pool."

Chris never told his mother about the actual sequence of events. He never discussed it with Pam. He couldn't comprehend why he had remained silent in the face of mortal danger.

This is not Chris's defining moment. It didn't change him. It didn't create a moment of before and after for him. But it revealed something strange about him. It was part, he assumed, of a sometimes embarrassing, sometimes unspeakably shameful, but random assemblage of bugs in his programming. He never imagined they might share a common cause.

Then he saw the documentary series called *The Keepers*. It recounted the unsolved 1969 murder of a nun, Catherine Cesnik, who had been a teacher at an all-girls Catholic high school in Baltimore. The series interviewed witnesses, now middle-aged women, who alleged that they were sexually abused while students at the high school. It raised the possibility that Cesnik had been killed after she began suspecting a priest at the school of perpetrating the abuse. These women described an odd constellation of personality quirks, fears, and behaviors that sounded familiar to Chris. They were his own. But here was the thing. These women, functional, intelligent adults now in their forties but with baggage eerily similar to Chris's, had reached adulthood *without any memory of the abuse.*

They could see the damage. They had forgotten the collision that caused it. But over the course of the documentary, the truth of the abuse they had suffered was revealed. Objective evidence confirmed that violence had been done to them. There could be no question. This was no case of false memories. They had succeeded at burying their memories of real but searing experiences so deeply, they found themselves scarcely able to retrieve them.

In the light of the stories these women told, Chris recognized for the first time the shape of the gaping wound in his own chest. It looked for all the world like he'd taken a bullet, a bullet shaped very much like the one fired into those women. But he couldn't remember the gunshot. The moment that defined him, if it existed at all, was lost to him.

One other detail about the documentary impressed Chris. It provoked in him an outsized response, a geyser of raw emotion that sent him fleeing the room where the TV was playing and left him sobbing. When he watched a second documentary, *Leaving Neverland*, the account of two young men who allege that as boys they were sexually molested by Michael Jackson, he experienced a similar sense of recognizing himself in those men. That film, too, triggered a tsunami of emotion.

For the first time in his life, Chris considered the possibility that, even though he couldn't remember it, an act of sexual violence might have been committed against him when he was six or seven years old. If so, that experience might account for the seemingly unconnected areas of brokenness he observed in himself. And if that were the case, he realized with a sense of relief one might not have expected him to feel at this moment, the embarrassment and shame he carried might not be necessary. It might not be deserved. He might go free.

But was it possible that such an event had occurred? Chris remembered that his dad, a homebuilder in the Midwest, had employed a construction foreman who was convicted many years later of molesting a twelve-year-old boy. Chris could remember this man visiting his home. He didn't remember this man hurting him.

Chris made an appointment with a counselor, looking for guidance on how to proceed. He never managed to retrieve any lost memory or locate a moment that might have inflicted lasting damage on his heart and mind. He did locate a series of lies programmed so deep in his psyche that they evaded detection for decades, even as they limited and tormented him.

"Men are dangerous," said one, so Chris avoided them.

"If you'd been good, this wouldn't have happened to you," said another down through the years, and so Chris had worked compulsively to appear good.

"If anyone finds out the truth about you, they'll stop loving you," said the most poisonous, and so Chris had hidden the truth about himself, discounting the commitment of those who did in fact love him, believing that any admission of imperfection would result in a fatal rejection.

Like vampires, lies like these turn to dust in the sunlight. When Chris, over the course of many counseling sessions, dragged the lies he'd believed into the open and examined them, he watched them shrivel, deprived of their force, and he found himself newly empowered to replace each one with a corresponding truth.

"Some men are dangerous. Not all. And you're not that six-year-old boy anymore."

"It's not your fault that this happened to you."

"The people who love you already know the truth about you. And they love you still."

The lies still echo. They have to be confronted each time with the truths. Chris is letting go of embarrassment and shame. He is learning to admit his disappointments, his weaknesses, and his mistakes. He is daring to come out of hiding.

We might not have a memory of a moment that defines us for several reasons. We might have buried a memory we once possessed because remembering causes us pain. But we might not remember the moment because we were too young when we experienced it, or too sick. Doctors say that few people remember their time in the ICU, perhaps because it's too traumatic, but also because they're too sick and sedated to make memories there. And the relatively new science of epigenetics reveals the startling fact that we can carry the trauma of previous generations in our genes, which means that the traumatic experiences of our ancestors can visit us through the makeup of our very cells.

Do you carry within you the damage — or, alternatively, the strength — of a moment you can't remember? Can you see the impact crater but not recall the moment of impact? Or do you recognize an inner treasure you own but don't remember the moment it was invested in you? What clues can you collect by examining the forensic evidence of your own heart and mind, your impulses and choices, your fears and drives? Perhaps understanding or healing are available even if knowledge of the lost moment is not.

If you suspect that such a moment exists, describe the evidence you observe in yourself. Write as much as you're able about the limp, the nature of the pain, the characteristics of the inexplicable superpower. Pay special attention to the unexamined statements you've embraced as truth but that might not be. Drag them into the light. Do they crumble to dust? If they do, leave them. Find the truth instead. Let it set you free.

Add your description of these mysteries to your collection of defining moments. Imagine the haunting characters that might rise from this dust.

Remember Kathy's refrain: "Before you can tell someone else's story, you have to understand your own."

If you've done the hard work encouraged by this chapter, you may have taken several important steps toward understanding your own story. And that understanding will serve you well as you search out the defining moments of the characters you build.

4.
Discovering a Character's Defining Moments

CHARACTERS START AT ZERO.

When a new character stands in the wings an instant before stepping onstage, the audience knows nothing. Characters arrive cloaked in complete mystery. We discover only what the storyteller shows us: The character's appearance. Their manner of speaking. Their habits. Their choices. Their secrets. Their lies. Their audacity. Their beauty. Their soul. And the gradual, progressive, scandalous revelation of a character's soul — the sacred striptease — rivets us.

But we only know what you, the storyteller, show us. And you can only show us what you know.

Having searched out moments that define us, the storytellers, we come now to the work of discovering the moments that define our characters. This work engages what we know of ourselves, what we know of other humans we've encountered, and what our imaginations conjure. It may involve searching the pages of a script or other text. It may demand research: a trip to the internet, to a buffalo ranch, to the Jet Propulsion Lab, or to Angola Prison.

It welcomes flashes of insight and inspiration, but it doesn't leave discovery to chance alone.

This work, while organic and creative, rewards discipline. We're more likely to discover the moment a character suffered a lasting wound if, instead of lying on the beach waiting passively for inspiration to strike, we ask the question, "When did this young mother suffer the wound that has left her unable to speak her mind and advocate for what she needs, even when her child's life hangs in the balance?" A question like that acts as a treasure map. It sets us digging where loot is likely to be buried.

But before I can ask such a specific question to guide my search for the moment when this young mother was wounded, I need to know that she bears this wound. I have to know she has a child. I'd like to know her name.

We've said that characters, if they resemble people, are infinitely complex. And we've said that omniscience about any character is impossible. What are the questions, then, that will lead us to what we must know about a character and that will create a context in which we can commence a meaningful search for their defining moments? Where can we find a treasure map to inform that search?

Over the years of our work telling stories, we've developed a set of strategies that give shape to our thinking about characters. These strategies help us ask a robust set of questions about a character and create space in which we can make unexpected discoveries about them. These strategies are not a formula. They're reminders to ask our character for her secrets and to listen closely as she makes herself known.

The Hero Questions

Years ago, in an article published in *Written By*,* the journal of the Writers Guild of America, we read about Bill Idelson and learned a great storytelling truth. Idelson was a prolific television writer and a two-time Writers Guild Award winner. The article told of the way Idelson mentored young writers at his home in Pacific Palisades. "What's a story?" he would ask them. And then, after they failed to provide an answer that satisfied him, he would tell them, "The story is the hero's struggle against the obstacle to reach the goal."

That simple definition of story provides invaluable clarity for the storyteller. All of the *Lord of the Rings* trilogy comes into focus. It's Frodo's struggle against the forces of Mordor to reach Mount Doom to destroy the One Ring. That definition works at the macro level of an entire television series or feature-length film. It also works at the micro level of every scene.

Playwright and screenwriter David Mamet has expressed the same idea in different words.† He says he asks of every scene he writes, "Who wants what from whom?" The "who" points to the protagonist of the struggle, the hero. The "wants what" points to the goal. And the "from whom" suggests the obstacle. A scene without one of these ingredients, Mamet wants us to understand, falls flat.

With these principles in mind, we collected a set of questions we ask about our characters when we first meet them. We've come to call this list the Hero Questions.

First on our list is an inquiry about the character's goal. We ask, *What does this character want?*

---

* Marsha Scarbrough, "Table Manners: How WGA award winner Bill Idelson mentors writers," *Written By*, November 2002.

† David Mamet, *Bambi vs. Godzilla: On the Nature, Purpose, and Practice of the Movie Business*, Vintage, 2008.

And because we understand that many of the most interesting characters change over the course of their struggle against the obstacle to reach the goal, we ask a second question. *How does this character need to grow and change?*

Because we want the audience to care about our characters and invest emotionally in them, we ask: *Why do we root for this character? How is this character like us?* We include with the questions examples of the sorts of qualities that have drawn us to root for characters in the past: *Flaws/quirks/nobility/humor/audacity/genius/drive/pain.* Alternatively, we might ask, "How is this character *unlike* me — but why do I root for this character anyway?"

Two more questions help us clarify our understanding of the story's stakes. *What terrible thing will happen if the character doesn't reach the goal?* and *What terrible thing will happen if the character doesn't grow and change?*

For the character driving the story, we ask, *What is the hero's initial plan to reach the goal?* since a hero who doesn't pursue a goal doesn't generate a story many of us want to watch.

And in fealty to Bill Idelson, we ask, *What are the major obstacles that stand in the way of the hero reaching the goal?* We approach this question not primarily in service to plot but first as a character question. What obstacles exist within the character that must be overcome if the hero is going to reach the goal? What obstacle would prove most challenging for this particular character? Which would prove most costly to the character and most demanding of change?

Next, we ask, *Why does the hero's initial plan fail?* This again is a question rooted not primarily in our interest in plot but in character. People tend to follow the path of least resistance. They plot the easiest route to reach their goal. Rarely do they purposely choose to take the most dangerous and demanding road, the one that will require more than they have to give. But the most interesting and exciting stories unfold, of course, on the most challenging paths. These are the paths we want our characters to take. And even they take the potholed, washed-out, bandit-haunted road only after they find the freeway closed. Only after their initial plan fails. Then they have to make a new, more desperate plan. These new plans demand more.

To remind ourselves to think along these lines, we ask, *What is the hero's last, desperate plan, why will it require the hero's growth, and why will it succeed or fail?* Our protagonist's struggle toward the goal intensifies. The plot thickens. But it thickens as a direct outgrowth of the character's struggle, not as a result of the storyteller's contrivances of plot.

The entire list of Hero Questions can be found in Appendix A. And though we call them "Hero Questions," they can be asked of villains, too, and every character in between.

Egri's Three Dimensions of Character

The author Lajos Egri, in his classic guide to dramatic writing,* delineates what he calls three dimensions of character: physiological, sociological, and psychological. Thinking about characters in these three dimensions leads to further important discoveries.

The physiological dimension prompts us to examine the character's physicality. How old are they? How tall? How strong? Are they healthy or ailing? What's their gender? Curly hair or balding? Dark skin or light? Have they lost a limb, or do they require a hearing aid? Any scars? How do they walk? What's their posture? How attractive do others find them?

---

* Lajos Egri, *The Art of Dramatic Writing: Its Basis in the Creative Interpretation of Human Motives*, 2nd ed., Touchstone, 1972.

The sociological dimension reminds us to consider the ways a character is shaped by interactions with other people. Were they raised by a single mom? A single dad? In foster care? By wolves? Where did they grow up? How much money did their family have? What sort of education did they receive? What style of parenting? Did they grow up with siblings? Did they suffer abuse? What grades did they earn? Who were their friends? How do they make their money today? How much do they make? What do they spend it on? What's their family situation today? Are they dating, married, divorced, or in a long-term relationship? Whom or what do they worship? What is their social status? Their political affiliation or orientation? What do they read, watch, and play?

The psychological dimension spurs us to think about the character's inner life. Are they an extrovert or introvert? How active or passive? What motivates them? What disappointments and frustrations do they experience? What do they fear? What do they long for? How smart are they? How honest? How Machiavellian? How creative? How patient? How brave? What about obsessions, compulsions, and neuroses?

By considering questions like these, we give ourselves the opportunity to notice our characters in multiple dimensions. We give our imaginations the chance to make unforeseen leaps.

Dr. Showers' Eight Character Traits

Our friend Sidney Showers, MD, is a pediatrician. She's also a smart and accomplished writer. She compiled a set of character traits that guide her thinking as she develops characters for her scripts. They provide additional opportunities to think about a character and glimpse unseen facets of the character's psyche. We now include them in our own development process with characters.

Dr. Showers asks eight questions:

1. **What is the character's drive?** This question seeks to understand an internal motor that lasts longer than the pursuit of a single goal. A goal is time-specific. A character must stop a killer asteroid from destroying the planet before next Tuesday afternoon at three. A drive precedes discovery of the asteroid and endures beyond its destruction. Our asteroid-hunter lives to protect people from unseen dangers. Frodo's goal is to destroy the One Ring. His *drive* is to side with good, no matter the cost.

2. **What is the character's goal or desire?** Like the first of the Hero Questions, this question seeks to name the concrete, immediate objective for the present story. The answer provides the starting point for the character's outer journey. By the end of the story, the hero will either reach this goal or fail to reach this goal in some conclusive way.

3. **What is the character's need?** Like the second of the Hero Questions, this question identifies the character's need to grow or to fill some significant lack. The answer provides the starting point for the character's inner journey through the story. It provides the audience with a sense that the character's soul hangs in the balance. If the character satisfies this need by the end of the story, the audience will feel a sense of triumph. If the character fails to satisfy this need, the audience will feel a sense of tragic loss.

4. **What is the character's genius?** We don't like to tell stories of unremarkable characters. Even the outwardly ordinary

characters who feature in our films, television, plays, and novels possess some extraordinary ability. It could be a high IQ, as with John Nash in the film *A Beautiful Mind*. But the character's genius may have nothing to do with IQ. Forrest Gump acknowledges, "I may not be a smart man," then he puts his finger on his superpower when he continues, "but I know what love is." Forrest Gump's genius is the purity and permanence of his love.

5. **What is the character's most closely guarded and/or most embarrassing secret?** This question assumes that everyone has a secret and recognizes that these secrets can motivate characters to sometimes dramatic or absurd actions to keep them. Secrets can also lend enormous intrigue.

6. **What is the character's weakness?** If most characters interesting enough to feature in a story have a genius, most also have a corresponding or offsetting weakness. Think of the mighty warrior Achilles and his infamous exposed heel. *A Beautiful Mind*'s John Nash is genius enough to invent game theory and win a Nobel Prize, but he also suffers from schizophrenia. The combination of strength and weakness contributes to the complexity of his character and the poignancy of the film.

7. **What is the character's flaw/sin/bad habit?** Showers explains that while she doesn't think of the character's weakness as a moral deficiency or failure, she does think of the character's flaw, sin, or bad habit as having a moral or ethical quality. It's Hamlet's indecision. It's the first two little pigs' lack of industry when they build their

houses out of straw and sticks. It's Ted Kennedy's Chappaquiddick.

8. **What is the character's redeeming trait?** Like the character's flaw, this quality often has an ethical dimension, this time an admirable one. It's the quality that can make us overlook a character's failings. It's the reason we give our friends a pass even when they behave badly, because we remember when they drove us to the ER in the middle of the night, or we know that secretly they're paying their mother-in-law's electricity bill. In *Forrest Gump*, Lieutenant Dan is merciless in blaming Forrest for saving him from death on the battlefield — but he's also fierce in defending Forrest from ridicule, and he remains Forrest's loyal friend over many years. In *The Godfather*, Vito Corleone commands a group of ruthless criminals — but he loves his family and will go to any lengths to protect them.

Thinking about a character in light of these eight character traits helps to round out our picture of a character, providing context in our search for the keys to the deepest and most comprehensive understanding of a character.

Hearing a Character's Voice

Characters speak. How they speak — their word choices, their colloquialisms, the way they string words together, the sorts of things they say and don't say — reveals much about them. Hearing and recognizing the character's voice can unlock for the storyteller, whether writer or actor, crucial access to the essence of the character.

We can't remember Forrest Gump apart from his distinctive manner of speaking. Or *Winnie-the-Pooh*'s Piglet, Eeyore, or Pooh. Or *Breaking Bad*'s Jesse Pinkman. Or Sean Connery's James Bond. Or Disney's Mickey Mouse. Chris can't separate his memories of his Grandma Riley, whom the family called G.R., from her "Whoo, doggies" and her description of a neighbor: "He was so cross-eyed, he could stand in the middle of the week and see both Sundays. We used to say one eye was going fishing and the other was digging worms."

When we adapted the nonfiction book *Actual Innocence* as a movie for television, we faced a very different character challenge. The book, written by Innocence Project cofounders Barry Scheck and Peter Neufeld along with Pulitzer Prize–winning columnist Jim Dwyer, told the stories of men convicted of crimes that DNA evidence later proved they didn't commit. They were legally guilty by virtue of their convictions but "actually innocent," a condition the law doesn't contemplate. Our job was to tell the stories of Dennis Fritz and Ron Williamson, two men in Oklahoma wrongly convicted of the rape and murder of a young woman named Debbie Carter.

We worked face to face with the book's authors, two of whom were also characters in the movie, but didn't have the opportunity to meet Fritz or Williamson. We didn't have access to their accusers. If we were going to give voice to these characters for two hours in a movie, we wanted more. Attorneys Scheck and Neufeld sent us boxes filled with thousands of pages of trial transcripts. We dug in and read. We unearthed gem after verbal gem, recorded verbatim by the court stenographer, that gave shape to our characters' voices and revealed much about them. We could not have imagined or written such lines.

The following scene opens the movie: The characters' distinct voices — in this case, the voices of jurors we never met — emerge word for word from the trial transcript:

```
FADE IN:

INT. JURY BOX - DAY
Twelve prospective jurors. Serious.
Sober. Midwest simple.

            JUDGE JONES (O.S.)
    The defendant is charged with murder
    in the first degree. If you find beyond
    a reasonable doubt that the defendant
    is guilty, can you consider each
    punishment, death, imprisonment for
    life without parole, or imprisonment
    for life? Mrs. Abbott?

                  ABBOTT
    I couldn't consider death. I could
    consider life without parole and life.

            JUDGE JONES (O.S.)
    Mrs. Lee?

                   LEE
    I think I can.

            JUDGE JONES (O.S.)
    Mr. Ballard?

                  BALLARD
    I feel the same way about it.
```

JUDGE JONES (O.S.)

Mr. Mann?

MANN

Yes.

JUDGE JONES (O.S.)

Mr. Likowski?

LIKOWSKI

I feel the same.

JUDGE JONES (O.S.)

Okay. Now, the same as who?

LIKOWSKI

Yes.

JUDGE JONES (O.S.)

You could consider each possible punishment?

LIKOWSKI

Right.

JUDGE JONES (O.S.)

Mrs. Flowers?

FLOWERS

If there's no doubt in my mind I could do all three of those.

JUDGE JONES (O.S.)

No reasonable doubt?

FLOWERS

No reasonable doubt.

JUDGE JONES (O.S.)

Mrs. Dobbins?

DOBBINS

No, the death.

JUDGE JONES (O.S.)

Mr. Black?

BLACK

Same, yes, sir, I agree with it.

JUDGE JONES (O.S.)

Okay. Now, agree with who?

BLACK

Whatever you said, yes, sir.

JUDGE JONES (O.S.)

Can you consider each of the possible punishments, each one, is that what you were saying?

A little hesitation.

BLACK

I didn't catch what you said.

But the old guy still smiles, ever helpful.

These distinctive voices do more than reveal quirky characters. They help dramatize the answer to the central thematic question the book and script address: "Why do juries convict innocent people?"

Later, when a witness named Jimmy Harjo testifies against Dennis, another distinct character voice emerges from the trial transcript, one we couldn't have created alone, but one that suggests a useful strategy for capturing the voice of any character, fiction and nonfiction alike. In this scene, Harjo recounts a conversation with Fritz that may or may not have happened, one that Harjo seems to think demonstrates Fritz's guilt.

INT. PONTOTOC COUNTY COURTHOUSE – DAY

JAMES HARJO, a small-potatoes burglar with a flair for drama, addresses jurors from in front of a board.

HARJO

It happened on Halloween night. Dennis and me, we was serving time in the county jail together. Dennis was sitting there at the table, so I asked him, I said, "What's you worried about?" And he said some guy named Gary Allen was going to testify against him that he seen him washing blood off him. Him and Ron washing blood early in the morning. That's what Gary Allen was supposed to testify.

Harjo awkwardly uncaps a marker.

HARJO

And so I asked Dennis, I was just playing around with him, and I said, "Dennis, do you have a water faucet?" And Dennis said no. So I put a little line.

Harjo draws a small line on the board.

HARJO

I can't hardly read or write, so I put a line where I can remember them, and I tried to write water. I could write water, you know. I can't write faucet, so I just put "water" and "f."

On the board, he writes "water f."

HARJO

Then I said, "Dennis, do you have a water hose?" And Dennis said no. So I put a line right there and I put a "water" again, and right there I put a "h-o-e," I guess that's how you write it.

Harjo scrawls more secret code, warming to this game.

HARJO

And I asked him if he knew Gary Allen. And he said no. So I put a little line right here.

(illustrating)

And I put "G-a-r-y" and I just put "A." And after that, you know, I just sat there and looked at him for a little bit. And I said every house's got water faucets. Jim Walters can build you a home in the Sahara Desert, and he'll build a water faucet with it. He said, "Yeah, yeah, there's one right behind our house."

Harjo seems to think this is a critical admission and gives the jurors time to absorb it.

HARJO

So I put a little X right here over that line. Now he's got a water faucet. And I asked him, I said, "Do you know Gary Allen?" He said, "No, I don't know him." And we just sat there for a little bit and then he said, "Yeah, yeah, I think I do." He said he used to live in the garage apartment right behind his house.

Harjo spreads his hands before the jury. Ta-da.

HARJO

So my mind right there, that made what Gary Allen said was true. Gary Allen seen them washing blood off each other in the back yard.

(pointing at Dennis)

He said he didn't have a water faucet -- then he said he did. Said he didn't have a water hose -- then he said he did. He said he didn't know Gary Allen -- then again he said, "I think I know him."

Harjo nails Dennis with his best Colombo "gotcha."

PETERSON

Then what did you say to him?

HARJO

I just said -- I said, "I think you're guilty, Fritz."

(marks board)

And there was a little "g" up there, like that, for guilty. I don't know how to write that. And he got upset.

```
Peterson jumps on that, eager for more.

                    PETERSON
          What happened? What happened next?

                      HARJO
          He got up, and he was walking back and
          forth. And he sat down in front of me,
          and I looked at him. We looked eye to
          eye. Man, that just, you know, a big
          old chill hit me, and I just looked
          at him. "Man," I said, "man, this guy
          really did do it." And I grabbed me a
          donut, and I went in my cell.
```

Harjo speaks in a manner unique to him, one shaped both by his sociology and psychology. We discovered that voice buried in thousands of pages of trial transcripts. That was a gift. If we needed to write additional lines of dialogue for Harjo not present in the transcript, we could sample the passages above to capture his voice and then channel it into additional lines that would match his idiosyncratic speech patterns.

It turns out it's possible to obtain a sample of any character's dialogue to use as a guide in this way, even one you create from whole cloth. Here's how.

Set aside a chunk of uninterrupted time to steep yourself in what you know of your character, the answers to the Hero Questions, your responses to Dr. Showers' Eight Character Traits, what you can say about the character's physiology, sociology, and psychology, and anything you know so far about your character's defining moments. Wrap yourself in your character's mind and body. Then start writing a rambling monologue from your character's point of view. Don't try to write dialogue for the script. Instead, unleash a rant or a stream-of-consciousness journal entry in your character's own hand, expressing the dreams, secrets, frustrations, ideas, grievances, arguments, justifications, hopes, and fears that ricochet inside your character's psyche. You may write much you can't use. But you will, if you let the words flow, find your character's voice. You will have a sample from which you can draw, like a tuning fork that will allow you to keep your character's voice true.

Beginning the Search for Your Characters' Defining Moments

Once you've spent time with your character asking and answering questions like the ones we've included above, you're ready to ask deeper questions about the moments that have defined, are currently defining, and in the future will define your character.

We think a good place to begin is with your answer to the second Hero Question: *How does this character need to grow and change?* Your response to this question will often point to something wounded, damaged, lost, or lacking in your character.

When did your character suffer this wound? How did your character incur this damage or experience this loss? Or when and how did this unsatisfied need emerge?

In the series *The Mysterious Benedict Society*, Tony Hale plays both the benevolent Mr. Benedict and his evil — or, to use Hale's term, "misunderstood" — twin, Mr. Curtain. "People aren't just born villains," the actor told us. "They're not born to be this dark. What nurtured this?" This is the kind of question all storytellers must ask.

The character work you've already done provides territory to explore. Sift through the first formative years of your character's life. Contemplate your character's family dynamics. Reflect on the pressures applied by peers and siblings. Did they experience misunderstanding, misguided parenting, abandonment, or abuse? Did they suffer hunger or the violence of war? Did they flee their home? Did someone they depended upon die? Did they come to believe a crippling lie? Was life too easy, and were they deprived of necessary opportunities to struggle and grow strong? Were they never told they were loved?

If you're working from an existing text — a script or a novel — mine for clues to a defining moment that is already present in or implied by the text. "You're grabbing onto the givens," says actor Joseph Barone. "Those are the things that are on the page." But what if the text lacks any accounting for your character's wound, damage, or need? According to Barone, "There are other things. It's either subtext or things that I'm going to get to make choices about. That's kind of the sausage-making of it all. Ultimately, my goal is to get to the point that is on the page."

Hale speaks of his exploration of the script as his "conversation with the writer." In this conversation, both writer and actor play a role in laying out the path of transformation — the arc — of the character. "Writers write the arc, and I sign up for the arc. But in order to do the arc, the muscle tissue has to find the right transitions. For me to jump from A to B, it has to find an organic bridge. It has to make sense to me. It has to ring true for me to get to B from A. And I think that's the connective tissue that hopefully I bring to the table. But many times I've read scripts and I'm like, 'Whoa, that turned a corner. In two pages, how did that happen? It didn't feel very human.' It's got to track on the page. The page is just so important."

You may make your characters and theirs arcs more human by looking to your own defining moments, one of which may serve as a model or inspiration as you imagine a defining moment for your character. If nothing from your own life serves, look to the lives around you, especially the ones you've observed at close range. And look to your imagination, which can fly beyond any territory you've inhabited or observed.

Ideas will occur. Call these "defining moment candidates." Collect as many as you can. Then, as with any candidate, ask questions, review the résumé, and check references. You're looking for a moment that creates the injury, damage, or need you've already identified in your character. It must also be one that rings true psychologically. One that results in lasting change. And one that owes its parentage more to things you've seen in life than to things you've watched on a screen. Moments sourced from real life offer the prospect of freshness; those sourced from the screen smell stale.

Once you've selected the moment, turn your imagination toward its details. Where did it happen? Who was present? What exactly transpired? What words were spoken? What was the nature of the injury? How terribly did it hurt in the moment? And afterward? What practical and emotional difference did it make in the life of your character? When your character looks back on this moment, how do they think about the before, and how do they think about the after? Have they told anyone about this moment? How have they described it? Why does it linger?

Bathed in the fullness of your character's defining moment, write down the story in a paragraph, like a short scene. Safeguard this written record. It is a key to understanding your character.

Extending Your Search for Your Character's Defining Moments

Some defining moments occur before the movie opens, the curtain rises, or the book begins. Others unfold in the middle of the story before our spellbound eyes. Still others burst into view at the story climax and constitute the big, noisy, emotional finish. Some longed-for moments never transpire, and we feel their presence only by their absence. And sometimes, the story's ending promises a defining moment still to come after the final fade-out, beyond our view but not our hope.

For now, let's continue looking into your character's past.

Our characters arrive on the scene not only wounded, broken, and in need but equipped with some combination of extraordinary strength, nobility, audacity, humor, drive, dream, or desire. Where did that genius or dream come from? When did it first make itself known to your character?

Explore your character's past for the moment they first discovered or flexed the muscle of their personal brand of strength or felt the tractor-beam tug of an enduring dream or goal. Immerse yourself in the scene. Take in its details. Pinpoint the moment of change. Write about it.

Finding More Defining Moments from Your Character's Past

During your preliminary development work on your character, you may have learned that your character is shaped by some bond or commitment they formed in their past, or by some deep and lasting emotional change, or by a discovery or decision they've made, or a secret they've buried and continue to protect. Delve into your character's past for the decisive moment at the root of this bond, emotional change, discovery, decision, or secret. Conduct an imaginative search until you find the defining moment, then write about it and add it to the ring where you keep all the keys you're collecting that unlock the deepest possible understanding of your character.

Considering the Impact of Moments That Define Generations or Peoples

It's no surprise that many who grew up in the U.S. during the Great Depression live with a different set of values and habits than do many who came of age during the 1960s. Both the Great Depression and the 1960s represent moments that defined their generations. So do the Civil War, World War I, World War II, the Vietnam War, Watergate, 9/11, and COVID-19. When looking for moments that define a character, consider the character's age and how they were affected by these generational defining moments. To what extent did the seminal moment of your character's generation shape them? Does it create a boundary that separates before from after? Understanding that different characters experience the same moment in unique ways, imagine how the big generational experience shaped your character individually. You may discover a defining moment that unlocks your understanding of your character.

The racial, ethnic, or religious group to which a character belongs can also exert a powerful influence on how they experience life in general and defining moments in particular. A white college student in 1960s Alabama would have experienced the civil rights movement very differently than a black college student at the same place and time. A Jewish character who survived the Nazi Holocaust will be forever marked by that experience in a way profoundly different from a Buddhist character who lived through that same moment in history in the mountains of Nepal. Chris drives back and forth between Los Angeles and San Diego nearly every week. His route takes him through Customs and Border Protection checkpoints set up on the freeways and roads leading north from areas near the U.S.–Mexico border. As Chris passes through those checkpoints, they barely register in his consciousness. But his experience of driving through those checkpoints would be radically altered if, instead of being a white, documented American, he were a brown, undocumented immigrant from Honduras. He wonders how the experience would change if he were a brown documented American. And that curiosity about how a character's racial, ethnic, or religious identity shapes them is exactly the sort of curiosity that can lead you to breakthroughs in your understanding of that character.

Looking to the Present for Defining Moments

Not all defining moments lie in the past, recalled in flashbacks or monologues. Many take place in the present. They pop before our eyes. We watch live as the character steps across the line that divides before from after.

The Godfather offers multiple examples of these defining moments unfolding in the present. We've described one transformative moment for the film's central character, Michael Corleone. When Michael guns down the police captain and the rival mafioso behind his father's shooting, we see the moment unfold in the present. We experience it at the same time Michael does.

Later, in another defining moment of intense irony, we watch in real time as Michael becomes the reigning Godfather by having all his rival mob bosses slaughtered while he stands in church, acting as godfather during the baptism of his sister Connie's baby.

The film ends with another defining moment that transpires in the present. This moment belongs not to Michael but his wife Kay. Connie has burst into the Corleone home in a rage to accuse Michael of killing her husband Carlo.

"And do you know how many men he had killed with Carlo?" Connie asks Kay. "Just read the papers. That's your husband."

Kay asks Michael if this is true. As described in the screenplay, "She looks directly into his eyes, he returns the look, so directly that we know he will tell the truth."

"After a very long pause," the script tells us, Michael says, "No."

Kay is momentarily relieved. But almost immediately, she watches as Clemenza, Neri, and others she knows to be mafiosos enter the house, gather around Michael, and pay him their professional respect. "Don Corleone," she hears Clemenza say.

"The smile fades from Kay's face," the writers tell us, "as she looks at what her husband has become."

In this defining moment, Kay makes a discovery. She learns who her husband is. And we know, even without watching the subsequent Godfather films, that her life and marriage have forever changed. We've watched her cross the boundary.

As director, Coppola understood how much changes in this moment. To help the audience appreciate what they're seeing, he visualized the separation created in this moment by using a door, just as he used doors to help him visualize Michael's passage from war hero to killer before the shooting at the restaurant. In this case, Kay watches from the kitchen as the *caporegimes* join Michael in his office to offer their allegiance. As soon as Kay "looks at what her husband has become," Michael swings the office door closed, hiding himself from her sight and closing off the possibility of honesty and intimacy between them. The doom falls.

In a story about a character who changes — whether for better or for worse — we should expect to see defining moments that take place in the present, creating moments that divide before from after, who the character was from who the character is now becoming.

Actors can look for these moments in the script. Finding them and forming a clear understanding of what changes in such a moment allows an actor to do two important things. First, having appreciated the significance of the moment, they can give it room to transpire within their mind and body, which will in turn give the audience the opportunity to feel in their own minds and bodies the weight of the moment. Second, understanding what has changed in such a moment for their character allows an actor to offer two manifestations of the same character. Before the moment of change, they can play the version of their character who has not yet experienced the change that moment will bring. Following the moment, they can play a version of their character who has undergone this change.

Without the benefit of a script that's already been written, writers doing the work of crafting a character-driven story can look at the overall path of growth that a character will take. They can locate the beginning point — "Who is this character when the story begins?" — and the ending point — "Who is this character when the story ends?" Between those poles, writers can imagine, shape, and describe the moments of incremental change through which the character will pass, one bit of change at a time, moment by defining moment.

Look at the character you're building. Who are they when the curtain rises? Who are they when the curtain falls? What forces and events reshape them along their journey from fade-in to fade-out? To help you locate those moments, consider the effects of the character's struggle against obstacles to reach their goal, especially those obstacles that challenge them at their point of greatest weakness, brokenness, immaturity, foolishness, or lack.

Writers and actors alike can allow themselves to be guided in their search by characteristics of defining moments:

- A grievous loss is suffered.
- A lasting wound is inflicted.

- A deep and lasting emotional change occurs.
- A moral or spiritual change takes place.
- A life-changing choice is made.
- A life-changing discovery is made.
- A profound lesson is learned.
- A birth or death occurs.
- A connection or commitment is made or broken.
- A dream or longing is awakened.
- Healing or growth takes place.

Writers: Imagine, craft, and write about the moments you discover. Actors: Take note of the moments you locate. Use your understanding of these moments to shape your script or your performance to allow the audience to witness the meaningful changes wrought by life upon your characters.

Looking to the Future for Defining Moments

Our characters arrive at a story's starting line having been carved by past moments. During the course of the story, additional moments redefine them in the present as they struggle before our eyes on the stage or on the screen. Still other moments take place after the audience exits the theater or cinema, closes the book, or powers off the TV. These moments we can only imply as hopes or dreads. They exist as possibilities. But they can nonetheless spring to life in the imaginations of our audience. Sometimes this happens by accident rather than design. A story so captivates the audience that it lives on in their imaginations long after the storytellers have gone home. This active audience involvement in imagining more than we've offered sometimes expresses itself in elaborate and impressive works of fan fiction. But some of what the audience imagines extending beyond the final fade-out happens by our design. We imagine a defining moment for our character that may happen after they pass out of our view. We imply the possibility. We encourage the audience to hope for or fear it.

Look at the trajectory of your character through the story. Will their journey of change terminate when the story ends, or will it continue? Have you created such momentum in the character arc that the audience can't escape its implications for the character's future? What do you imagine will happen next? How will it further the character's growth? How will it redefine them?

The series *Breaking Bad* ends with the death of one lead character after a long journey of transformation and with the rebirth of another. In the last moments of the episode finale, Jesse Pinkman, like Lazarus, emerges from the grave. And as he drives away in a liberated El Camino from the site of his worse-than-death forced labor, we imagine a future for him. For Jesse, we sense, that future will have to include a massive redefinition of self. We don't know the particulars. But we know Jesse hasn't finished his journey. Defining moments loom. We hope for him. This is no accident. Both the writer and the actor understand and encourage our hopes.

Think about the character you're building. Where do they stand at the end of the story? Where is their trajectory likely to carry them? How do you want the audience to feel about that trajectory? What do you imagine comes next?

Canadian acting teacher David Rotenberg has written about the importance of a character's expectation of what comes next: "You cannot understand how a man lives his life until you understand what he thinks is going to happen to him when he dies. Change what he thinks is going to happen to him after he dies, and you have quintessentially changed the character."

Actors and writers will gain a fuller understanding of a character by imagining the moments of growth and transformation that may lie in the character's future, even though those moments are not guaranteed. Search for those moments. Use the list of characteristics of defining moments above to spark your thinking. Write about the moments you discover, or imagine them with such vivid detail that they live inside you and gain through you the opportunity to find life in your audience.

Looking Forward from Here

You've discovered and imagined in rich detail moments that have defined your character in the past, that redefine your character in the present, and that may further define your character in the future. Hold onto each of these moments. Some will find their way explicitly into the story. Others will shape and inform your understanding of the character in subtler but important ways that allow you to know what a character will or will not say or do when confronted with the extraordinary challenges the story will present. And some may fall away entirely, replaced by new discoveries that ring truer to the character you're building. In Chapter 6, we will examine the practical ways you can incorporate your newfound knowledge of your character's defining moments to enrich your storytelling. But first we need to consider how our understanding of defining moments applies when we work not with fictional characters but with characters based on real people.

5.
Discovering a Nonfiction Character's Defining Moments

DEFINING MOMENTS OCCUR IN THE WILD. REAL PEOPLE EXPERIENCE THEM.

Readers who have engaged in the exercises found in Chapter 3 of this book will already have discovered more than one defining moment in their own real lives. Writers, actors, directors, journalists, and even historians who work with the stories of real people as opposed to fictional characters can gain crucial insights into these nonfiction characters and how to make their stories comprehensible, relatable, and dramatic by uncovering their defining moments.

The Defining Moment That Makes Sense of a Notorious Warrior King

Between the year 1200 and his death in 1227, Genghis Khan emerged from a traditional nomadic life on the steppes of Northeast Asia to gain dominance leading his Mongol riders to violent conquest of lands that stretched thousands of miles from east to west. Cultural anthropologist Jack Weatherford writes in the introduction to his *New York Times* bestselling biography

Genghis Khan and the Making of the Modern World, "In twenty-five years, the Mongol army subjugated more lands and people than the Romans had conquered in four hundred years." An apparently barbaric medieval warlord without written language, Genghis Khan somehow united the Mongol tribes and rode roughshod over China and Mongolia, across Asia into the Middle East, and as far west as Eastern Europe. "On the modern map," writes Weatherford, "Genghis Khan's conquests include 30 countries with well over 3 billion people." Under Genghis Khan's direction, his warriors slaughtered soldiers and civilians numbering possibly into the millions. He also collected countless tribes and countries into a united empire; he established the first diplomatic and commercial contacts between Europe and China; he created a massive free-trade zone; he set up a postal system that served his sprawling lands; he established a rule of law that included international law and diplomatic immunity; he outlawed torture; he insisted on religious tolerance. But over the centuries since his death, his personal life has remained opaque. Little was known about the man himself. As recently as 1998, when Weatherford set out to discover the man Genghis Khan, "as a historical person he was still missing." But then a treasure trove of new information became accessible. The author worked with a dedicated team to plumb the depths of the character who was Genghis Khan and find his "true face." His task was to make it possible for a modern reader to understand this brutal, brilliant, and utterly alien warlord from the distant past.

How did he do it?

He collected and assembled the facts from his years of research roaming the lands of the Mongol Empire. But he did more. He identified individual moments that shaped not only the course of Genghis Khan's life but also his character. In his telling of the warlord's life, Weatherford used these moments as anchor points. They became for author and reader alike keys at last to unlocking the secrets of the great Khan.

One event above all others illustrates Weatherford's discoveries and their power to present the man at the center of his story. It comes at a time of duress for Genghis Khan, who was then still fighting to unite the Mongol tribes under his rule and still went by his given name, Temujin. He was on his way to marry the daughter of Ong Khan, his mentor and the ruler of the Kereyid tribes, when he learned that Ong Khan, fearing the growing power of Temujin, planned to betray him. Temujin and his entire family were in mortal danger. Separated from his own army, he was forced to flee into the wilderness with a small band of allies. "The events that followed," writes Weatherford in language that unambiguously marks the episode as a defining moment, "became legendary among the Mongols as the greatest trial and triumph in Temujin's life."

Temujin and his band of fugitives arrived on the shores of Lake Baljuna, a muddy and desolate body of water far from any source of food or shelter. Only nineteen men remained with Temujin. All had exhausted themselves in their long escape. All now faced starvation.

Then a wild horse appeared.

Temujin's brother Khasar chased and killed it. The men ate its meat. Weatherford writes:

> With little to comfort them or offer encouragement for the future, the exhausted men seized upon the appearance of the horse as a supernatural gift that offered them more than just food for their empty bellies. As the most important and honored animal in the Mongol world, the horse solemnized the occasion and served as a sign of divine intervention and support. The horse symbolized the power of Temujin's destiny, and its

> sacrifice, as before any major battle or *khuriltai*, not only fed the men, but further empowered Temujin's Spirit Banner. With only the muddy water of Baljuna to drink at the end of the horse-flesh meal, Temujin Khan raised one hand to the sky, and with the other he held up the muddy water of Baljuna in a toast. He thanked his men for their loyalty and swore never to forget it. The men shared in drinking the muddy waters and swore eternal allegiance to him. In the retelling of the episode in oral history, it became known in history as the Baljuna Covenant, and acquired a mythic aura as the lowest point in the military fortunes of Temujin Khan but also as the event out of which the identity and form of the Mongol Empire would arise.*

Weatherford uses this moment to explain a phenomenon he calls unique in history: "None of Temujin's generals deserted him throughout his six decades as a warrior. In turn Temujin never punished or harmed one of his generals."

The moment on the shores of Lake Baljun exerted a lasting effect upon the man who would later gain the title Genghis Khan and upon the men who would fight for him across his expanding empire, often to their own deaths.

The author does more than sift through a treasure trove of data and provide his readers a flat historical account. Instead, he captivates readers by telling them a story. And the anchors of that story are Genghis Khan's defining moments, which Weatherford brings into sharp focus, making sure we grasp their significance.

Harnessing a Defining Moment from the Lives of Abraham and Mary Todd Lincoln

The 2012 film *Lincoln*, written by Tony Kushner and directed

* Jack Weatherford, *Genghis Khan and the Making of the Modern World*, Broadway Books, 2004.

by Steven Spielberg, humanizes the person of Abraham Lincoln, played by Daniel Day-Lewis in an Oscar-winning performance. It does this in part through Lincoln's homespun humor and almost compulsive digressions into folksy anecdotes. But the film gains enormous emotional resonance by tapping into a single defining moment the president shares with his wife Mary: the death of their son Willie at the age of twelve in the White House.

Lincoln tells a straightforward story about the title character's efforts to pass the 13th Amendment through the House of Representatives, outlawing slavery in the United States. The moral and spiritual stakes for the country couldn't be higher. But the story's plot centers on legislative process, strategy, and negotiation. The story's heart lies elsewhere. From all the events in Abraham Lincoln's life, screenwriter Kushner plucks one to highlight.

On the evening the First Couple hosts a White House reception for Washington's elite, a critical opportunity for Lincoln to line up support for the amendment, Mary, played by Sally Field, takes refuge in the bedroom where her son died three years earlier on the night of another White House reception. Lincoln finds her sitting on Willie's bed.

The screenplay reads:

> Mary holds a framed photograph: an image of Willie, 12, handsome, bright-eyed, confident.
>
> Lincoln crosses to the window.
>
> MARY: My head hurts so. (beat) I prayed for death the night Willie died. The headaches are how I know I didn't get my wish. How to endure the long afternoon and deep into the night.
>
> LINCOLN: I know.

MARY: Trying not to think about him. How will I manage?

LINCOLN: Somehow you will.

MARY: (sad smile) Somehow. Somehow. Somehow . . . Every party, every . . . And now, four years more in this terrible house reproaching us. He was a very sick little boy. We should've cancelled that reception, shouldn't we?

LINCOLN: We didn't know how sick he was.

MARY: I knew, I *knew*, I saw that night he was dying.

LINCOLN: Three years ago, the war was going so badly, and we had to put on a face.

MARY: But I saw Willie was dying. I saw him —

He bends and kisses her hand.

LINCOLN: Molly. It's too hard. Too hard.

Mary stares up at him, her face heavy and swollen with grief.

We gain access to the grief, regret, pain, and humanity of this iconic couple when they touch the awful moment of loss that redefined them.

Later in the film, Kushner deploys the same defining moment a second time when Lincoln and Mary argue about their oldest son Robert's desire to serve in the Union Army. Lincoln has decided to enable that desire and has found Robert a position serving as adjutant to General Grant. Mary fears the worst.

MARY: The war will take our son! A sniper, or a shrapnel shell! Or typhus, same as took Willie, it takes hundreds of boys a day! He'll die, uselessly, and how will I ever forgive you?

Lincoln begs her to see it from Robert's point of view. The desire to serve is natural, Lincoln says, and they mustn't stifle it.

> MARY: And if I refuse to take the high road, if I won't take up the rough old cross, will you threaten me again with the madhouse, as you did when I couldn't stop crying over Willie, when I showed you what heartbreak, *real heartbreak* looked like, and you hadn't the courage to countenance it, to help me —

Husband and wife talk over one another, Mary furious that her husband objected to the way she grieved, furious that he abandoned her to grieve alone, until Lincoln finally reveals to Mary what he experienced in the terrible aftermath of Willie's death.

> LINCOLN: I couldn't tolerate you grieving so for Willie because I couldn't permit it in myself, though I wanted to, Mary. I wanted to crawl under the earth, into the vault with his coffin. I still do. Every day I do. Don't . . . talk to me about grief.

Two flesh-and-blood humans, Abraham and Mary Todd Lincoln, evoke our compassion and our recognition that they are *humans like us* through the revealing power of a defining moment that has, by their testimony, wrought a permanent emotional change in both of them. And we will argue it is these scenes more than any others in the film that elevate these characters and create space for Daniel Day-Lewis and Sally Field's incandescent performances.

Moments That Redefine Entire Groups of Real People

Is it possible for a single shared experience to redefine a large group of real people in a way that permanently sets them apart from all others?

HBO's 2001 limited series *Band of Brothers* explores one such moment for a company of paratroopers during World War II. The moment is D-Day. The series presents this moment that so completely defines a group of men that it permanently divides soldiers who experienced it from those who didn't.

Unlike *Saving Private Ryan*, which depicts the experiences of soldiers landing on the beaches of Normandy on D-Day, *Band of Brothers* follows the travails of Easy Company, a legendary unit of paratroopers in the 101st Airborne Division dropped in France behind enemy lines the night *before* the D-Day invasion.

The paratroopers have trained together for two years leading up to their first combat action. Now in England, on the eve of D-Day, they board transport planes and make the trip across the English Channel. Over France, they experience the terror of anti-aircraft fire that rocks their plane and blasts others from the sky, sending whole platoons, along with Easy Company's commander, to fiery deaths before they ever reach the drop zone. The remaining men of Easy Company leap from their plane into the night sky, stripped by the wind of their weapons and targeted by searchlights and machine guns as their chutes blossom and they descend into war. Once on the ground, they risk more enemy fire to find one another in the dark of the battlefield and race together through hostile country to their objective at Brécourt. There they undertake a brazen attack on a superior force of German artillery troops shelling the Allies landing on Utah and Omaha Beaches. They succeed at silencing the deadly German guns. Following that initial victory, they're thrown almost immediately back into a bloody street-to-street battle, during which they take the strategic town of Carentan. Bloodied and exhausted but expecting a German counterattack, they take up a defensive position on the high ground outside Carentan. Then they encounter a large, dug-in

German force backed by German tanks. Once again, they fight to a costly victory as, at every point, men from Easy Company are maimed and killed even as they display great heroism and devotion to one another.

This concentrated series of intense battlefield experiences surrounding D-Day wins the unit a presidential citation and represents a defining moment for the survivors of Easy Company. It binds them to one another. It also separates them from everyone else. When they return to England to regroup, the army sends them replacement paratroopers to replenish their numbers. So dramatically have the original members of Easy been changed by their experience in Normandy, however, that the veterans have enormous difficulty welcoming the new men. Likewise, the new men have enormous difficulty earning a place among the veterans. This clash between those who have been redefined by combat and those who haven't headlines an entire episode in the ten-episode series. It's called "Replacements." Only because of the lasting effects of the defining experience of combat in Normandy on an entire group of nonfiction characters do the conflict and storyline make sense.

Moments That Transform Real People into Heroes

We might suspect that heroes only exist in movies. We might doubt that we'll find them among the actual men and women who inhabit the complicated and morally ambiguous world that we, too, inhabit.

Azam Ahmed, *New York Times* bureau chief for Mexico, Central America, and the Caribbean, tells the story of one such true hero in a story published in 2020.*

* Azam Ahmed, *New York Times*, "She stalked her daughter's killers across Mexico, one by one," December 13, 2020.

Back in 2014, Miriam Rodríguez lived in the town of San Fernando, Mexico. A cartel that called themselves the Zetas dominated the town, intimidating local residents and police alike. When her daughter Karen, just twenty years old, disappeared, Miriam concluded that the Zetas had kidnapped her. Miriam paid them ransom more than once, borrowing and spending every penny she could get her hands on to save her child.

Ahmed writes:

> With every payment, a new hope sparkled for Mrs. Rodríguez. And with every failed bid to reclaim Karen, she fell further into despair.
>
> Hope is a toxin that poisons many families of the missing. They either purge it and try to move on from their loved ones, or they sustain it, and it destroys them.
>
> Mrs. Rodríguez, already separated from her husband, moved in with her older daughter, Azalea. One morning, a few weeks after the last payment, she came downstairs and told Azalea that she knew Karen was never coming back, that she was most likely dead. She said it matter-of-factly, as though describing her sleep.
>
> She told her daughter that she would not rest until she found the people who had taken Karen. She would hunt them down, one by one, until the day she died. Azalea watched as her mother's sadness hardened into resolve and her hope gave way to revenge.
>
> Her mother was a different person after that.

This is the unmistakable mark of a defining moment, the boundary between the person before and the person after. In Ahmed's telling, the new person did things the old Miriam never would have done as she hunted the people responsible for taking her daughter.

> She cut her hair, dyed it and disguised herself as a pollster, a health worker and an election official to get their names and addresses. She invented excuses to meet their families, unsuspecting grandmothers and cousins who gave her details, however small. She wrote everything down and stuffed it into her black computer bag, building her investigation and tracking them down, one by one.

In the end, she discovered the details of Karen's abduction and murder. She brought about the arrests of ten Zetas, nearly every individual involved in her daughter's killing. In one case, she chased down a fleeing suspect on a bridge at the U.S.–Mexico border and held him at gunpoint for close to an hour until police arrived to arrest him.

Her crusade achieved much of the justice she sought for her daughter. It made Miriam famous. And it turned her into a threat and a target.

"On Mother's Day, 2017," writes Ahmed, "weeks after she had chased down one of her last targets, she was shot in front of her home and killed. Her husband, inside watching television, found her face down on the street, hand tucked inside her purse, next to her pistol."

When the *New York Times* podcast *The Daily* retold the story,* they positioned the moment of Miriam's transformation from despairing victim to justice warrior as their act one cliffhanger. They recognized its significance, made sure their audience recognized it, and harnessed its narrative and emotional punch as the

* *The Daily*, "Please, Give Me Back My Daughter," February 3, 2021.

central turning point in their broadcast.

Strategies to Locate Defining Moments in the Lives of Real People

Your source material will determine where you begin your search for a nonfiction character's defining moments. You may be an actor coming onto a project with a script already written. Or you may be a writer adapting a biography or some other kind of source material. In other cases, you may begin without an existing text but with access to the living person.

When You Have an Existing Text

Begin by searching the text for defining moments that have already been dramatized or described. Remember that all defining moments have a before-and-after quality. This quality can serve as a helpful clue in your search. Sometimes, the language of the source material makes it obvious: "Neighbors report that Ruth was never the same after the alien abduction."

You may also find clues to additional moments to which the text only alludes. Sometimes, the text won't unveil the moment but will provide a tantalizing clue: "It's unclear what happened to Ruth that summer night in 1972, but neighbors report that after she returned from the desert, she was a different person."

The full list of the characteristics of defining moments found in Chapter 2 can provide you with further guidance. Does the source material describe, allude to, or infer a birth or death that makes a lasting difference, as the death of Willie did for Abraham and Mary Todd Lincoln? Do you encounter any indication of a grievous loss, a lasting wound, or an enduring emotional, moral, or spiritual change? Do you find reference to a time a lifelong bond formed, as it did on the shores of Lake Baljuna between the soon-to-be Genghis Khan and his future generals? What about a life-changing discovery or decision? Does the text suggest a profound lesson that is learned, a dream that awakens, or healing that takes place? Pull on any one of these threads and see if it leads you to a defining moment.

If your search of the script or source material fails to turn up moments that make satisfying sense of a nonfiction character, you may want to dig deeper. When we adapted the nonfiction book *Actual Innocence*, we drew all we could from the book itself. We still had questions. We flew to New York and visited the headquarters of the Innocence Project. We interviewed the authors and met Innocence Project interns and staff. They sent us home with a box filled with the thousands of pages of trial transcript that we searched for more clues. All of that additional research revealed unexpected insights into the real people who were the subjects of our script that enriched our work with nuance and complexity.

When You Lack an Existing Text

Many times we begin our creative search for the essence of a nonfiction character without benefit of a script or biography. If our subject is alive, nothing can substitute for time spent with them in conversation and observation.

These encounters rank among the greatest joys of our creative work. We've visited a state penitentiary to spend time with inmates and guards. We've had serial conversations with an Olympic coach as he raced to qualify his team for the most dangerous sport in the Winter Olympics. We've talked to champion athletes, an undercover Drug Enforcement Administration agent who spoke to us by phone from the midst of a clandestine operation, a woman who spent many anguished years looking for her abducted daughter, and a journalist who befriended Lee Harvey Oswald's mother following his assassination of John F. Kennedy and spent Christmas with her to get her story. In every case, we learn things we never could have invented.

Interviewing the subjects of our storytelling, however, presents challenges. Our work would be so much easier if the subjects carried with them a catalogue of the moments that have defined them, as clear and accessible as a résumé. They don't. Many people resist telling us about their most pivotal experiences. Those experiences continue to cause pain. Or embarrassment. Or anguish, or confusion. Many more people simply don't know which moments have defined them. Recall the work each of us had to do to discover our own defining moments. Remember what it cost in emotional capital.

When you meet with a living human person on whom you hope to base a character, you will encounter these barriers. The finer points of interview technique lie beyond our expertise and the scope of this book, but regardless of your skill as an interviewer, an understanding of the role played by character-defining moments can guide your interview strategy, providing rich targets for inquiry.

As you prepare your questions, draw on what you already know about your subject — their history, their aspirations and accomplishments, the struggles they've faced — to zero in on key relationships, fateful decisions, extraordinary abilities, obsessive drives, crippling wounds, and life-changing discoveries or innovations. Plan to inquire about the moments of before and after associated with them. Ask when your subject first embraced the dream they now chase. When did they first recognize their unusual love for snowboarding or their unique skill with the harpsichord? When did their interest in human rights abuses become an obsession? When they shifted from victim to crusader, what was the turning point? At what point did their courage overcome their fear? Where and when did that fear originate?

Review the list of characteristics of defining moments found in Chapter 2. Let those characteristics shape your questions. Probe your subject about losses and wounds, decisions and discoveries, especially if you already have reason to believe that any of these things has played an important role in shaping them. Expect that many people will downplay and avoid telling you stories of their defining moments. Many of us avoid revealing ourselves at this depth. Many shield our most important stories from view. Dig to unearth them with the perseverance of a stubborn archeologist.

Open an additional line of inquiry into your subject's response to the generational defining moments through which they have lived. How was their life changed by the assassination of Martin Luther King Jr. or the racial justice protests of the summer of 2020? To what extent did the Great Recession or the COVID-19 pandemic reshape them? To what extent are they shaped by having a grandparent who endured the Holocaust or generations of ancestors who lived as enslaved people?

Your understanding of defining moments will inform your conversations and maximize your chances of obtaining revealing and meaningful responses. In this way, you will discover keys to unlocking a deep understanding of a nonfiction character.

* * *

You can sharpen your interview skills by practicing with someone you already know. Before your conversation, think about what you know about this person: strengths, dreams, wounds, goals, relationships, commitments. Prepare questions, as explained above, that will allow you to probe for defining moments that might lurk behind those characteristics. With practice, you'll learn how to ease into an honest conversation, how to invite vulnerability by offering your own, and how to ask direct questions even though they make you uncomfortable because you fear they'll make your conversation partner uncomfortable. You'll strengthen your ability to uncover defining moments.

6. Enriching Your Storytelling with Defining Moments

IF CHARACTERS ARE THE PRODUCTS OF A HALF-DOZEN DEFINING MOMENTS, and if we manage to locate each of those moments for our characters, how exactly do we employ our knowledge of those moments to enrich our storytelling?

Some defining moments we will translate into vivid, unforgettable scenes that play out before our eyes. Our characters will allude to other pivotal moments. Still others they will recount in rambling, revealing speeches. But many moments will remain submerged within the heart and mind of the writer or actor, deepening their understanding of what a character will say and do, how they'll say and do it, and why they'll say and do it. They'll add richness and complexity we can't achieve any other way.

Each of us will work hard to discover these moments for our characters and to craft the stories that capture them. We must trust that no defining moment, whether expressed in some explicit form on screen or not, goes to waste.

Enlisting Defining Moments That Occur Before the Story Begins

Author Lajos Egri uses the term *point of attack* to describe the instant the dramatist chooses for the curtain to go up on a play. It's the place the storyteller begins the telling. Of course, the characters' lives extend into the past that precedes the point of attack. Characters exist before the curtain rises, before the film fades in. But the *telling* of any story begins at the point of attack.

How do we harness moments that have occurred before this formal beginning?

A Flashback from Ratatouille

Sometimes we send cameras into the past to shoot the scene and present it as a flashback. Instead of telling it, we show it.

The 2007 Pixar film *Ratatouille* makes powerful use of a brief flashback to bring a defining moment that occurred before the film began onto the screen in the present. Having heard glowing reviews of the food at Gusteau's restaurant in Paris, fearsome food critic Anton Ego returns to the establishment he once panned to taste a dish cooked, unbeknownst to him, by the rat chef Remy. When the skeptical Ego takes his first bite of Remy's ratatouille, his eyes widen in surprise — and something more. The audience plunges into Ego's memory. They witness the moment that Ego, as a young boy, first tasted his mother's ratatouille. Then the audience is sucked back into the present at Gusteau's, experiencing Ego's reconnection with a moment that holds obvious power over him still. In this brief flashback, the film douses us in a moment that speaks universally of innocence and home and food and comfort, giving a sense both of where Ego's love of food began and just how far he has wandered. All this happens without explanation, and all in a matter of seconds. We don't learn everything about the past moment, but we nonetheless feel all of its impact on the character. Anyone who has seen the film remembers these few seconds. And this brief flash of insight revolutionizes the way we feel about Ego, transforming him from villain to something closer to a friend and ally.

Stories Retold

A flashback isn't the only way to bring a defining moment from the past into the present. In many memorable instances, a character recounts the moment in dialogue. And while this strategy would seem to defy the filmmaking dictum "Show, don't tell," these speeches often pack surprising emotional and dramatic power.

How is that possible?

Maybe what we're witnessing in these riveting cases is dialogue serving as a form of action. At the climax of the 2011 film *Darkest Hour*, Winston Churchill, on the eve of war with Hitler's Germany, delivers his stirring "We shall never surrender" speech to Parliament. The speech rallies MPs to his side, ready at last to engage with the enemy threatening their survival. One of Churchill's flummoxed opponents, blindsided by the response to the speech, asks, "What just happened?"

Lord Halifax knowingly responds, "He just mobilized the English language — and sent it into battle."

Sometimes writers manage to mobilize language and send it into battle, a clear example of words exerting their mightier-than-the-sword power in the retelling of a defining moment. And through these speeches, actors sometimes work their magic with such mastery that we in the audience are rendered breathless and spellbound. August Wilson's stage play *Ma Rainey's Black Bottom* accomplishes this feat.

Midway through the play, Levee, a black musician in Ma Rainey's band, appears to kowtow to Sturdyvant, a white record company executive. Levee's fellow musicians mock him without mercy, suggesting that he fears the white executive. Provoked beyond all measure by their mocking, Levee unloads with an impassioned speech.

> LEVEE: Levee got to be Levee! And he don't need nobody messing with him about the white man — cause you don't know nothing about me. You don't know Levee. You don't know nothing about what kind of blood I got! What kind of heart I got beating here! (He pounds his chest.)

Here he reaches into his past to tell the story of a moment that neutralizes their mockery but simultaneously reveals a moment that defines him.

> LEVEE: I was eight years old when I watched a gang of white mens come into my daddy's house and have to do with my mama any way they wanted. (Pauses.) We was living in Jefferson County, about eighty miles outside of Natchez. My daddy's name was Memphis . . . Memphis Lee Green . . . had him near fifty acres of good farming land. I'm talking about good land! Grow anything you want! He done gone off of shares and bought this land from Mr. Hallie's widow woman after he done passed on. Folks called him an uppity nigger 'cause he done saved and borrowed to where he could buy this land and be independent. (Pauses.) It was coming on planting time and my daddy went into Natchez to get him some seed and fertilizer. Called me, say, "Levee you the man of the house now. Take care of your mama while I'm gone." I wasn't but a little boy, eight years old. (Pauses.) My mama was frying up some chicken when them mens come in that house. Must have been eight or nine of them. She standing there frying that chicken and them mens come and took hold of her just like you take hold of a

mule and make him do what you want. (Pauses.) There was my mama with a gang of white mens. She tried to fight them off, but I could see where it wasn't gonna do her any good. I didn't know what they were doing to her . . . but I figured whatever it was they may as well do to me too. My daddy had a knife that he kept around there for hunting and working and whatnot. I knew where he kept it and I went and got it. I'm gonna show you how spooked up I was by the white man. I tried my damndest to cut one of them's throat! I hit him on the shoulder with it. He reached back and grabbed hold of that knife and whacked me across the chest with it. (Levee raises his shirt to show a long ugly scar.) That's what made them stop. They was scared I was gonna bleed to death. My mama wrapped a sheet around me and carried me two miles down to the Furlow place and they drove me up to Doc Albans. He was waiting on a calf to be born, and say he ain't had time to see me. They carried me up to Miss Etta, the midwife, and she fixed me up. My daddy came back and acted like he done accepted the facts of what happened. But he got the names of them mens from mama. He found out who they was and then we announced we was moving out of that county. Said good-bye to everybody . . . all the neighbors. My daddy went and smiled in the face of one of them crackers who had been with my mama. Smiled in his face and sold him our land. We moved over with relations in Caldwell. He got us settled in and then he took off one day. I ain't never seen him since. He sneaked back, hiding up in the woods, laying to get them eight or nine men. (Pauses.) He got four of them before they got him. They tracked him down in the woods. Caught up with him and hung him and set him afire. (Pauses.) My daddy wasn't spooked up by the white man. Nosir! And that taught me how to handle them. I seen my daddy go up and grin in this cracker's face . . . smile in his face and sell him his land. All the while he's planning how he's gonna get him and what he's gonna do to him. That taught me how to handle them. So you all just back up and leave Levee alone about the white man. I can smile and say yessir to whoever I please. I got time coming to me. You all just leave Levee alone about the white man.

(There is a long pause. Slow Drag begins playing on the bass and sings.)

SLOW DRAG: (Singing.) If I had my way If I had my way If I had my way I would tear this old building down.

Chadwick Boseman delivered this searing speech in the 2020 film version of *Ma Rainey's Black Bottom*. His posthumous Oscar nomination for his work in the role of Levee owes in no small part to that speech and the retelling of a defining moment.

The Value of Undisclosed Past Defining Moments

The action film *Twister* shot in Oklahoma during the spring of 1995. It stars Helen Hunt and Bill Paxton as two tornado-chasing meteorologists who risk their lives to place a package of scientific instruments they've dubbed Dorothy inside a killer tornado. They hope to use the data these instruments will transmit from the core of the cyclone to help them to predict tornadoes, providing people in the paths of these dangerous storms earlier warnings and saving lives. Michael Crichton and Anne-Marie Martin wrote the original screenplay. Joss Whedon and Steven Zaillian did additional work on the script. When Universal Studios and Warner Bros. jointly greenlit the project, they chose to rush it into production, understanding that they needed to shoot among the Oklahoma farm fields in the spring to match the year's most active time for tornadoes. If they waited until all parties were satisfied with every detail of the script, they would need to wait an entire year before they could shoot again in springtime.

At the time *Twister* went into production, Chris was managing the script processing department at Warner Bros. His department had typed the script for the studio and was supplying physical copies of the script to Steven Spielberg's Amblin Entertainment, the production company making the movie, as well as Universal and Warner Bros., the studios releasing the picture. Because the script was still being written, producers Ian Bryce and Kathleen Kennedy wanted to have a script typist on set with the writer — who was, by now, scribe Jeff Nathanson, who would go on to pen *Catch Me If You Can* and the live-action *The Lion King*, among many other titles. Bryce phoned Chris at the studio, explained what he needed, and asked if Chris had someone he could send to Oklahoma. Chris thought the assignment sounded like fun, so he decided to send himself.

Two days later, on location in a muddy field forty minutes outside Ponca City, Oklahoma, Chris found close to three hundred cast and crew at work shooting the film. They were about ten days into the shoot when he arrived. It was a massive operation, with a caravan of picture cars careening down country roads and across farm fields in pursuit of tornadoes. Actors played scenes while cowering in roadside ditches as truck-mounted jet engines blasted them with wind.

The script had Helen Hunt's character, Jo — along with her partner Bill, played by Bill Paxton — taking increasingly wild and unreasonable risks to position Dorothy in the path of onrushing tornadoes. On set and in dailies, Chris watched Hunt and Paxton chase their tornadoes and shout their lines over deafening jet blasts. He saw in Hunt's character Jo evidence of more than just scientific curiosity or altruistic concern for the safety of a generic populace. Some defining moment lurked in her past, something that drove her to take these mad risks.

But here's the thing. As Helen Hunt was playing her role, she didn't know what Jo's defining moment was. Because the scene hadn't yet been written.

A member of the crew reminded Chris that the current script contained a note to the effect that a scene would be written later to reveal Jo's backstory. It wasn't yet written, the crew member explained, because the writer needed to move forward with the scenes scheduled for shooting in the days immediately ahead, and the backstory sequence wouldn't shoot anyway until the end of May, several weeks away. What that delay failed to address, however, in the view of the crew member, was the fact that an actor would want to know her backstory now because that knowledge would impact the rest of her performance.

Think about what that crew member's insight reveals. The performance of an actor, future Oscar-winner Helen Hunt, no less, required an essential ingredient that in this case was missing. She needed to know her backstory. She needed to know the defining moment that gave rise to her obsessive need to fight the demon of tornadoes. The reason she needed this knowledge? *Because it would impact her performance in every other scene.*

Let's try a thought experiment. Imagine a scenario in which that defining moment is written as a scene and present in the script from the beginning of shooting. It captures a powerful, traumatizing encounter Jo has with a tornado in her childhood, one that redirects the course of her life from that moment forward. Knowledge of that moment then shapes Helen Hunt's performance every day of shooting during the month of April. Imagine further that when May comes, the film is far behind schedule and they're forced to cut the backstory scene. They never shoot it. The audience never sees it.

Would Hunt's performance as Jo the tornado hunter still benefit from the actor's knowledge of the defining moment? It is difficult to imagine that it wouldn't.

This is the power of the undisclosed defining moment. Knowledge of such moments informs and deepens the work of every writer or actor who possesses it, whether or not that moment is played explicitly on screen.

Tony Hale told us about a recent experience voicing a character in an animated production, a boy defined by a traumatic past. "When I allowed myself to really think about this situation and what this boy has been through, and I did the line, you could tell that it was different. You could tell in the booth that it was different. Then you ask yourself, 'Why am I not doing this more? Why am I not diving in more?' And I think it's just out of self-preservation. Out of just not wanting to go down there. But the older I've gotten, I've allowed myself to go down that path a little more. It's really useful because when I think about those markers in a character's life, when I do tap into them or I do really spend the time almost daydreaming about them, I think it does bring you to a deeper level of finding a character."

Subtext, attitude, mood, emotional complexity, motivations, and choices can all flow from writers and actors armed with a knowledge of a character's past defining moments—whether or not those moments are disclosed to the audience.

Enlisting Defining Moments That Occur in the Present

Defining moments aren't limited to the past. In story after story, they blossom in the present and constitute many of a narrative's most dynamic and consequential scenes. The 1997 epic *Titanic* illustrates the use of defining moments that unfold in the present.

When we meet the character of seventeen-year-old Rose, she's in crisis. Her mother, desperate to stave off bankruptcy, has pressed Rose into a loveless engagement with Cal Hockley, the self-absorbed heir to a giant fortune. More than eighty years later, the centenarian Rose will characterize her mindset as she boarded the unsinkable luxury liner:

> It was the ship of dreams . . . to everyone else. To me it was a slave ship, taking me back to America in chains. Outwardly I was everything a well-brought-up girl should be. Inside, I was screaming . . . I felt like I was standing at a great precipice, with no one to pull me back, no one who cared . . . or even noticed.

Seeing no way out of a life that seems to her unlivable, Rose makes her way to the ship's fantail, climbs over the railing, and prepares to jump. Jack intervenes and pulls her away from the precipice, back toward life.* The scene plays out in the present, and the audience experiences it with the characters. We feel not only the drama and danger of the moment but also the meaningful change that occurs. Jack and Rose meet. They connect. Rose's life reverses course. Both characters step across the line from before to after, and we watch it happen.

The work of writers grows clearer and sharper when they recognize the nature of a moment like this one. Seeing the moment coming, they set it up before they arrive at the moment itself, showing the audience the condition of the character in their before state. Then they craft the scene to capture the actual moment of change. They render it precisely for the audience, showing them the pivot, allowing them to feel its significance. They follow that pivot with evidence of the changed character, showing who the character becomes after the change.

The work of actors, like that of writers, grows more purposeful and revealing when they recognize they're playing a defining

---

* The moment of Rose and Jack's meeting is described more fully in Chapter 2.

moment. They know and can show who their character is before the moment of change. They can portray the actual moment of stepping across the before-and-after boundary. And they can apply their understanding of the redefined character to their performance thereafter.

Titanic offers additional defining moments that take place in the present, demonstrating how these present-tense moments can aid effective storytelling.

After he calls Rose back from the brink of self-destruction, Jack recognizes that while she has chosen not to end her life, she hasn't yet freed herself from the relational anchor that threatens to drag her back into fatal despair. The free-spirited Jack implores Rose to leave Cal and join him instead. Unable to believe that choice is possible for her, she refuses. In fact, she begs Jack to leave her alone. And then she returns to her suffocating life.

Sometime later, Jack stands on the bow of *Titanic*, looking forward alone. A voice calls out behind him.

"Hello, Jack," says Rose. "I changed my mind."

She's chosen hope and freedom. She's decided to disentangle herself from Cal and connect instead to Jack. This new bond is dramatized in a memorable scene with Jack and Rose on the bow of the ship.

The screenplay describes what happens next:

> He presses her gently to the rail, standing right behind her. Then he takes her two hands and raises them until she is standing with her arms outstretched on each side. Rose is going along with him. When he lowers his hands, her arms stay up . . . like wings.
>
> Slowly he raises his hands, arms outstretched, and they meet hers . . . fingertips gently touching. Then their fingers intertwine. Moving slowly, their fingers caress through and

around each other like the bodies of two lovers.

And in case we've missed the nature of the seismic change in Rose and in her relationship with Jack, the script tells us:

> Jack and the ship seem to merge into one force of power and optimism, lifting her, buoying her forward on a magical journey, soaring onward into a night without fear.

These are the words of a writer who recognizes the defining impact of this singular moment on his character and who makes unmistakable to every reader — every collaborator in the making of the film — the meaning of this moment. At the stern of the ship, Rose chooses not to die. Here at the bow, she demonstrates she has chosen to live. It happens in the present, before our watching eyes.

From this moment flows Rose's decision to ask Jack to draw her wearing the priceless Heart of the Ocean necklace and to place the drawing, the necklace, and a note in Cal's safe in his stateroom. But not before she says to Jack of his drawing, "Date it, Jack. I want to always remember this night." A signal that she and her screenwriter recognize that on this night, her world has changed. To be clear, this scene in the stateroom doesn't represent a new defining moment. Instead, it provides further evidence that highlights the change that already happened at the ship's bow.

This romantic sequence, beginning with the defining moment at the bow, is the emotional midpoint of the film. In the script, it's only a few pages later that the ship collides with the iceberg, the midpoint of the external, physical storyline and an additional defining moment for Jack and Rose, and for every passenger and crew member on *Titanic.* Because of course the luxury liner's collision with the iceberg changes everything about the voyage and the lives of those aboard in ways that can never be undone.

An epic, breathless action sequence ensues as passengers, all of our main characters included, scramble to escape the sinking ship. Again and again, Rose chooses Jack and the life he represents. Even when she has the opportunity to board a lifeboat without Jack, she leaves the boat to rejoin him, confirming in "the cauldron of the third act" — a term we learned from producer Peter Guber — the decision she made at the midpoint.

But then we reach the bittersweet climax of the movie. *Titanic* has sunk, and Jack and Rose swim in the frigid North Atlantic water, freezing to death as they await lifeboats that fail to return. When Rose seems on the brink of giving in to hypothermia, Jack encourages her to keep hoping and fighting.

"You're going to get out of this," he tells her. "You're going to go on and you're going to make babies and watch them grow and you're going to die an old lady, warm in your bed. Not here. Not this night. Do you understand me?"

And then, as if he understands the power of a vow to create a new and urgently needed defining moment for Rose, Jack says, "You must do me this honor . . . promise me you will survive . . . that you will never give up . . . no matter what happens . . . no matter how hopeless . . . promise me now, and never let go of that promise."

> ROSE: I promise.
>
> JACK: Never let go.
>
> ROSE: I promise. I will never let go, Jack. I'll never let go.

Another defining moment that plays out in the present, and we get to experience it in all its bittersweet intensity.

But almost immediately, the commitment Rose has just made will be tested. With hypothermia draining the life from her, she dozes off. She only wakes up when a lifeboat returns at long last seeking survivors. She attempts to awaken Jack to alert him to the possibility of rescue.

> She touches his shoulder with her free hand. He doesn't respond. Rose gently turns his face toward her. It is rimed with frost.
>
> He seems to be sleeping peacefully. But he is not asleep.
>
> ROSE: Oh, Jack.
>
> All hope, will and spirit leave her.
>
> She closes her eyes. She is so weak, and there just seems to be no reason to even try. And then . . . her eyes snap open.
>
> ROSE: I won't let go. I promise.
>
> She releases him and he sinks into the black water. He seems to fade out like a spirit returning to some immaterial plane.

This instant seems to represent a further defining moment, a death and a separation. From the time Jack called Rose away from suicide on *Titanic*'s fantail until now, he has been the force at work on Rose, calling her to life, saving her. Only with Jack does Rose have life. But now she separates from him and is left alone to save herself, if she will. Her next action reveals how much she's changed through the series of defining moments that have unfolded in the present, one after another, in a chain of growth that has transformed her from the helpless, hopeless fiancée who was ready to cast herself into this cold sea:

> Rose rolls off the floating staircase and plunges into the icy

water. She swims to Chief Officer Wilde's body and grabs his whistle. She starts to BLOW THE WHISTLE with all the strength in her body.

The writer first imagines each of these moments. The actor embodies them. The audience experiences them. This is the beating heart of cinema.

And then they're reunited in a vision of the transcendent future. Paradise restored.

How Defining Moments Interact with Story Structure

If defining moments play such an important role in storytelling, it's fair to ask where they fit in the shape of the overall narrative. Do defining moments play a role in story structure? Is it possible that defining moments can help us build the overall narrative structure?

Story structure has to do with the selection and arrangement of events in a narrative. Where do we begin the telling? What happens in the middle? Where do we end? The structure of feature films, and the structure of television episodes, builds around a finite number of anchor points. They give movies and television episodes their shape, help maintain audience interest, and contribute to a story's meaning. In movies, we commonly call the beginning of a story act one, the middle act two, and the end act three.

In our own writing, we've distilled the essence of feature screenplay structure down to eight points* that help us describe the shape of a movie:

---

* For a more detailed expression of these eight structural anchor points, see Appendix B, The Eight Essential Story Points.

1. The Opening
2. The Upsetting-the-Applecart Moment (more commonly called the Inciting Incident)
3. The End of Act One
4. The Beginning of Act Two
5. The Midpoint
6. The End of Act Two (frequently an All-Hope-Is-Lost Moment)
7. The Beginning of Act Three
8. The Story Climax

Do the defining moments we've identified in *Titanic* line up with any of these anchor points?

The first moment we recount above takes place at the aft railing of the ship when Jack calls Rose away from suicide and establishes a connection with her. We suggest that this moment represents the end of act one, the third of the eight structural points.

The next defining moment we describe — Rose's decision to leave her fiancé and join Jack, followed shortly by the ship's collision with the iceberg — represents the midpoint of the film, the fifth of the eight structural points.

The final pair of moments — Rose's promise to Jack that she won't let go, followed shortly by her separation from Jack and her determined action to blow the whistle and call back the lifeboat so that she can live — represent the climax of the film, the eighth and final structural point.

In the case of *Titanic,* at least three of the eight structural anchors consist of defining moments. Is this unusual? To what extent do others films employ defining moments to anchor their structure?

The Opening

The first of what we call the Eight Essential Story Points* is the opening. The first few pages of a screenplay and the first minutes of a film bear one overriding burden: to capture the attention of the audience. Failing that, nothing else matters because no one will be watching. In addition to gaining attention, the opening will often introduce the main character, the world of the story, and its tone.

The Fellowship of the Ring, the first film in the *Lord of the Rings* trilogy, opens with a spectacular battle scene. During the battle, the evil lord Sauron loses possession of the One Ring, an amulet that allows him to reign over all of Middle Earth. He loses this ring to the human king Isildur. In the history of the powerful ring at the center of the epic tale, this surely represents a defining moment.

The Return of the King, the third *Lord of the Rings* film, likewise begins with a defining moment. In this case, it's a fateful fishing expedition during which the hobbit-like Déagol discovers the lost ring at the bottom of a river and is then killed by his cousin Sméagol, who seizes the ring. Thus begins his devolution into the tortured character Gollum. This event creates a moment of before and after for Sméagol, for the ring, and for all the people of Middle Earth.

---

* We distilled these eight structural points during the early years of our work pitching to and writing for Hollywood studios. They are not our invention. We determined them by observing many films that connected with broad audiences and simply describing the pattern we observed. We can lay them side by side with Blake Snyder's fifteen beats and the structural schemas found in Robert McKee, Syd Field, Chris Vogler, and others and find substantial overlap. That is to be expected. All of us are describing the same pattern we find in the data. Vogler's work, drawing on the writings of mythologist Joseph Campbell, demonstrates that this pattern can be found not just in Hollywood films but in myths that persist in societies around the world, irrespective of both time and geography. We were drawn to a list with as few elements as possible because we are practitioners, not theorists, and we needed a wieldy tool that wouldn't constrain our creativity or reduce our storytelling to a formula but rather would help us shape our pitches and scripts.

The Upsetting-the-Applecart Moment

The second of the eight story anchors, the inciting incident or upsetting-the-applecart moment, represents the moment when the story sparks to life. Something happens that, in Robert McKee's words, "radically upsets the balance of forces" in the protagonist's life. A problem, challenge, or opportunity presents itself. In mythological language, the hero receives a call to adventure.

In *The Fellowship of the Ring*, the 111-year-old Bilbo Baggins, guardian of the One Ring since he took it from Gollum in an earlier story, Tolkien's *The Hobbit*, vanishes from his birthday party and sets out one final time for the country of the elves, but not before leaving the Ring to his nephew Frodo. When the Ring passes into the hands of Frodo, the protagonist of *The Lord of the Rings*, it radically upsets the balance of forces in his life, marking him as a target for Sauron's death-dealing servants the Nazgûl and leading inescapably to Frodo's eventual quest to carry the Ring to Mount Doom, deep in Sauron's realm, to destroy it. Thus, this defining moment for Frodo doubles as the inciting incident for the film.

The End of Act One

The end of act one constitutes the third of the eight story anchors. Here the protagonist often finds there's no turning back to life before the inciting incident. They can only press forward, face every obstacle, grow, and risk everything in an effort to reach the goal. Only then can McKee's balance of forces be restored. Often, it feels at this point that our hero is caught in a trap or shot out of a cannon.

In *Titanic*, it's the moment when Jack pulls Rose back from suicide and a bond forms that redirects both of their lives.

In the audacious and darkly comic 2019 film *Jojo Rabbit*,

which bills itself as "an anti-hate satire," ten-year-old protagonist Jojo Betzler is a pint-sized Nazi wannabe in World War II–era Germany. His imaginary friend, it so happens, is Adolf Hitler. Adorable little Jojo does all he can to fashion himself into a good Nazi but admits to his imaginary friend Adolf, "I don't think I can do this."

The audience hopes Jojo is right. They're not disappointed. Because Jojo, as it turns out, is a terrible Nazi but a pretty decent little human being.

So what happens at the end of *Jojo Rabbit*'s first act? Jojo, still hoping to grow into a respectable Nazi, discovers a secret panel that leads to a hidden compartment in the wall of his deceased sister's bedroom. When he explores the compartment, he finds someone living there, a seventeen-year-old girl named Elsa. Startled, Jojo flees. Elsa chases him and overtakes him when he falls on the stairs. Jojo, terrified, asks if she's a ghost. No, she says, she's something worse. She's a Jew.

Appalled, Jojo tells her she can't be here. But the self-assured Elsa tells him, "Well your mother invited me so I suppose that makes me her guest."

It's a double discovery for the little Nazi fanboy from which there can be no turning back. A Jewish girl lives in his house. And his mother is a secret anti-Nazi activist. You can hear the trap snapping closed on Jojo. These twin discoveries upend his understanding of his life. And this first meeting with Elsa initiates a friendship that will doom and displace his Nazi fantasy. This moment is both a structural anchor for the film and a defining moment for the protagonist.

The Beginning of Act Two

What about the fourth structural waypoint? If act one ends with the hero being caught in a trap, act two often begins with the hero making a plan to escape the trap. Viewed differently, if the end of act one brings the protagonist's goal into sharp focus, act two begins with the protagonist formulating a plan to reach that goal.

The 1998 film *The Truman Show* stars Jim Carrey as Truman, the unwitting star of a reality TV show. Unbeknownst to him, Truman has spent his entire life on the world's largest soundstage, living among actors who pretend to be his family and friends. It's the world's most popular show.

Throughout the first act, Truman picks up on clues that something may be wrong with his world. These discoveries escalate, until he has an eerily intimate encounter on a city street with a homeless man whom he recognizes as his dead father. This man, this actor, may be trying to communicate something important. Before the two can talk, anonymous pedestrians whisk the homeless man away. Truman gives chase, but the pedestrians seem to conspire to block his path. The mysterious stranger disappears, leaving Truman caught in a trap at the end of act one, locked in the mystery of his fabricated life.

Act two begins with Truman acting on a new plan. He tells both his mother and his wife about the strange sighting of the man who appeared to be his late father. He's begun to seek the truth. He descends to his basement, to a private closet where he keeps a poster advertising the island destination of Fiji. He also keeps a woman's sweater, which he now removes from a garment bag and presses to his nose, inhaling the scent of . . . someone.

Here the screenplay, written by Andrew M. Niccol, flashes back to a defining moment from Truman's past, the defining moment that anchors and motivates all of Truman's actions that follow. It also gives the audience something concrete and meaningful for which to hope.

We see Truman during his college days. We watch as he meets "an ethereal-looking young woman" named Lauren. In a series of short scenes that work together like a single action or moment, we see a genuine bond form between Truman and Lauren, culminating in a furtive, whispered exchange during which she confesses that her name is not Lauren, but Sylvia. For the first time in his life, Truman connects to someone real. The two kiss. Then Sylvia discloses the secret everyone has kept from him.

> SYLVIA: Everyone's pretending, Truman. You think this is real? It's all for you. A show. The eyes are everywhere. They're watching you — *right now.*

An actor, a middle-aged man, arrives to break up the encounter. He claims to be "Lauren's" father and drags her away, apologizing for the young woman's behavior. She's schizophrenic, he claims. Truman won't see his daughter again. They're moving to Fiji.

And like that, Truman's one true person, his first and only true love, vanishes from his world.

Truman's memory of this defining moment from his past crashes into his present at the beginning of act two, shaping his plan and driving him forward through the second act in pursuit of a future that he hopes will be the opposite of his past. It becomes the dividing line between before and after.

The Midpoint

The midpoint represents the fifth of the eight structural points. In a feature film, the second act constitutes about half of the entire movie. In a two-hour film, that means act two lasts about an hour. With no structural support in the middle, that long second act can sag. It can lose tension and, more to the point, interest. To provide shape to this hourlong second act, renew audience interest, reenergize the protagonist's quest to reach the goal, and create the opportunity for different sorts of scenes in the second half of act two than filled the first half, writers have come to rely on a midpoint that spins the story in a new direction.

This spinning of a character's story in a new direction sounds like the natural habitat of defining moments. And so it is.

In *The Godfather*, it's at the midpoint that Michael Corleone guns down Sollozzo and McCluskey.

In *Room*, it's at the midpoint that Jack and Joy make their escape.

In *Jojo Rabbit*, it's at the midpoint that Jojo bonds with Elsa. No longer does he want her out of his house. No more does he see her as subhuman. He forges a letter that he pretends comes from her fiancé Nathan but reveals Jojo's new desire. In it, Jojo pretends that Nathan writes, "I need you to stay alive. Thank God you are being taken care of by that kid, who I must say is a remarkable young man. Beyond his years. And brave too." Jojo has passed from before into after.

The End of Act Two

In a story with an "up ending," one in which the lead character either reaches the goal or grows in some way the audience recognizes as essential, the end of the second act represents the lowest point. Very often, it's a moment when all hope seems lost.

In *The Fellowship of the Ring*, it's at the end of act two that the wizard Gandalf is dragged to his apparent death in battle with the fiery Balrog, leaving the fellowship broken and Frodo feeling that his quest to destroy the One Ring and save Middle Earth has become hopeless. From this, there can be no going back. Another before-and-after frontier has been crossed. Another defining moment.

In *Jojo Rabbit* at the end of the second act, Jojo's free-thinking mother is hanged by the Nazis for defying the Reich. Not only is this a moment of emotional devastation for Jojo, it also spells the end of any possibility that he will ever become a true Nazi.

In *The Godfather* at the end of act two, Don Corleone's son and heir apparent Sonny is murdered by a rival mafia family. At the funeral home of Bonasera, the undertaker who in the opening of the film asked a favor of the Godfather, men bring in Sonny's body. The script describes what happens next:

> They carry the corpse to one of the tables in the embalming room.
>
> Then Bonasera turns to see another man step out of the darkness somewhat uncertainly. It is Don Corleone.
>
> He walks up to Bonasera, very close, without speaking. His cold eyes looking directly at the frightened undertaker. Then, after a long gaze:
>
> DON CORLEONE: Well, my friend, are you ready to do me this service?
>
> Bonasera nods. The Don moves to the corpse on the embalming table; he makes a gesture, and the other men leave them alone.
>
> BONASERA: What do you wish me to do?
>
> DON CORLEONE: (staring at the table) I want you to use all your powers, all your skill, as you love me. I do not want his mother to see him as he is.
>
> He draws down the gray blanket.
>
> Bonasera lets out a gasp of horror at what he sees: The bullet-smashed face of Sonny Corleone.

This moment of his firstborn son's death redefines Don Corleone's life and plans. It demolishes his hopes that he can safeguard his family. In the words of screenwriters Coppola and Puzo, "one feels that just for a second he loses all physical strength." The strongman has been rendered impotent. This is both a defining moment and a structural linchpin of the film, the end of the second act.

The Beginning of Act Three

If the protagonist suffers a devastating setback at the end of act two, the only way forward for them in the third act is to rise from the ashes and make a new plan. But this new plan will come at a cost. In a story where the lead character undergoes inner growth, the new plan will rely on that growth and call it into action.

In *The Godfather*, in the immediate wake of Sonny's death, the previously unyielding Don Corleone says to Hagen, his consigliere, "I want no inquiries made. No acts of vengeance." He pauses. "Consigliere, arrange a meeting with the heads of the five families . . . This war stops now."

This is a new Vito Corleone. In a single moment, his son's death has changed him. He plots a path into the future that is profoundly different than the one he has pursued until now. And whether Sonny's death and Vito's making of a new plan represent two distinct defining moments or a single defining moment and its aftermath, *The Godfather* demonstrates how a defining moment can put a stake in the ground that anchors a film's structure at the end of act two and the beginning of act three.

The Story Climax

A story crescendos in what Blake Snyder calls "the finale" and Robert McKee calls "the story climax." It's the big finish. The final showdown. The hero reaches or fails to reach the goal in some ultimate way. The main character demonstrates definitive growth — or a final failure to grow. The film's narrative question is conclusively answered.*

This territory seems ripe for defining moments.

In *Titanic*, the story climaxes when Jack dies — surely a defining moment both for him and for Rose — and when Rose subsequently releases him and blows the whistle, choosing to fight with all her remaining strength to live. In addition to serving as the film's big finish, it is for Rose her most defining of defining moments.

In *The Shawshank Redemption*, the A story climaxes when our protagonist, the innocent convict Andy Dufresne, makes good his escape from Shawshank Prison by tunneling out of his cell and swimming through a sewer pipe to a nearby river and freedom. This moment anchors the film's structure and answers the narrative question, "Will Andy ever get out of Shawshank?" But it does more. It dramatizes a monumental defining moment for Andy's character. His friend Red remembers Andy and his exploits like this:

> RED: When I picture him heading south in his own car with the top down, it makes me laugh all over again . . . Andy Dufresne, who crawled through a river of shit and came out clean on the other side.

You can hear the before-and-after language in Red's line, language that addresses not just an outward physical journey but an inner moral or spiritual trek. Here the story climax and the character's

---

* In storytelling, the narrative question is the foremost question the story poses. If someone tries to change the channel in the middle of a movie, it's the question that drives us to say, "Wait, I want to know what happens." *Titanic* asks the narrative question, "Will Rose be saved?" Once the narrative question is conclusively answered in the story climax, the tension dissipates. The storytelling ends soon. Otherwise, it wears out its welcome.

most consequential defining moment coincide.*

Each of these defining moments, no matter their role in supporting the film's structure, play out before the wide eyes of a spellbound audience and demonstrate how storytellers harness present-tense defining moments to build the tales they tell.

Enlisting Defining Moments That Will Occur in the Future

The 1976 film about the Watergate scandal, *All the President's Men*, takes an oblique and unexpected approach to its story. The film doesn't crescendo at the buzziest and most obvious event, the resignation of Richard Nixon from the U.S. presidency. Instead, it climaxes years earlier, at the moment reporters Bob Woodward and Carl Bernstein finally convince the executive editor at *The Washington Post*, Ben Bradlee, after harrowing fits and starts, that they've uncovered a bona fide White House scandal.

The moment turns as Bradlee speaks to Woodward and Bernstein:

> BRADLEE: Look, you're both probably a little tired, right? (they nod) You should be, you've been under a lot of pressure. So go home, have a nice hot bath, rest up fifteen minutes if you want before you get your asses back in gear — (louder now) — because we're under a lot of pressure, too, and you put us there — not that I want it to worry you — nothing's riding on you except the First Amendment of the Constitution plus the freedom of the press plus the reputation of a hundred-year-old paper plus the jobs of the two thousand people who work there —

* This is not yet the end of the film, however. That's because *The Shawshank Redemption* tells the intertwined stories of two men, Andy *and* Red. It asks two narrative questions: "Will Andy ever get out of Shawshank?" and "Will Red embrace hope?" The rest of the film, following Andy's escape, builds to the climax of Red's storyline and answers his narrative question.

Bradlee's speech answers the film's narrative question: "Will Woodward and Bernstein succeed at uncovering the truth at the heart of Watergate?" They will. But, interestingly, they haven't yet. And Bradlee concludes with words that point to future defining moments:

> BRADLEE: (shooing them off) Move-move-move — What have you done for me tomorrow . . . ?

The film ends with Nixon taking the presidential oath to begin his second term, the one he won with the help of a series of political dirty tricks and "all the president's men." A cascade of *Washington Post* headlines follows, each announcing the arrest or conviction of one of those men, culminating in the resignation of Nixon himself.

That defining moment for the protagonists, for Nixon, and for the country, the "what have you done for me tomorrow" moment of a president's public and permanent downfall, is not dramatized in *All the President's Men*. It is only presaged. It is a defining moment yet to be. And yet the gravity of its future existence exerts an irresistible pull on the present, drawing us toward that inevitable future defining moment that invests the present with its significance.

* * *

Actors, writers, directors, editors, cinematographers, production designers, and composers all play roles in the presentation of characters and their stories. Each of us engage with characters who have undergone moments that have redefined them in the past, who undergo moments that redefine them in the present, and who will undergo moments that will further redefine them in the future. Gaining an understanding of the significance of those moments allows each of us to use our particular art to bring the impact, emotion, nuance, and complexity of those moments into focus for the audience.

Actors: Look at the list of defining moments you've divined from what is written in the script. Add the defining moments that you've developed that don't appear explicitly in the script. How will you allow your knowledge of your character's past defining moments to inform and energize your performance in each of your scenes? How will you allow your recognition of a defining moment that happens in the present, onstage or onscreen, to inform and energize your performance before, during, and after that pivotal moment? How will your knowledge of a future defining moment that might occur after the end of the episode, movie, or play infect the present, especially the story's ending?

Writers: Look at the list of defining moments you've developed for your protagonist. Which moments from the past will a character retell in the present? Which won't receive mention but will inform the words, choices, and actions of your character? Which will unfold in the present? Lay your defining moments alongside the Eight Essential Story Points described in this chapter and catalogued in Appendix B. Do any seem to serve as anchor points for the structure? Does story structure as expressed in the Eight Essential Story Points suggest any additional defining moments you have yet to discover? Which defining moments belong to the future? How can your knowledge of future moments inform the present, especially your story's ending?

7. Beyond Building Characters

How recognizing defining moments helps us understand
the books we read, the wine we drink,
the companies we run, the patients we treat,
the students we teach, and the people we love

IN THE PRECEDING CHAPTERS, WE'VE SEEN HOW DEFINING MOMENTS CAN help storytellers build characters. What else might this magic key unlock?

If it's true that each of us is to a remarkable degree the product of a handful of pivotal experiences or decisions that have redirected the course of our lives, how might this insight provide a Rosetta Stone for understanding the real people all around us and the choices they make under pressure? How might it illuminate the source of the failings and the key to unlocking the untapped strengths of the people who work for us and the organizations we populate or lead? How might it equip the readers of novels and biographies, along with theatergoers and cinephiles and Netflix watchers, with a kind of X-ray vision into the souls of the characters who enthrall them? How might it equip teachers with a deeper understanding of their students and healthcare professionals with healing insight into their patients? And how might it change our relationships with the people we love?

Vineyards and Vintages

Living in California, we visit wineries in the great wine-producing regions of Santa Barbara County, Paso Robles, Napa, and Sonoma. Tasting the wines is part of the pleasure of visiting a winery, of course, but we've discovered that much additional enjoyment is derived from the stories the winery staff tell when pouring the wines.

The staff at Denner Vineyards, an award-winning winery in the hills west of Paso Robles, tell a story that links the origins of the winery with the name of one of their most popular wines, the Ditch Digger. Founder Ron Denner, they tell visitors, owned the Ditch Witch dealerships in four Western states, selling trenching and other "underground construction" equipment. According to the Denner Vineyards website, "After traveling the state for years searching for the perfect piece of dirt to grow grapes that would produce highly-acclaimed wines, Ron Denner finally found exactly what he was looking for in the far western reaches of Paso Robles in 1997." At that point, as the story goes, he converted his Ditch Witch earnings into Denner Vineyards, planting the hillsides with the best vines and eventually producing a wine he calls Ditch Digger, a blend of Grenache, Syrah, and Mourvèdre grapes. A recent vintage of Denner's Ditch Digger scored a rarefied 95 points from multiple leading critics.

The wine is great. The story is charming. But it isn't especially compelling—until you hear the detail we'd missed on our first visits.

During our most recent trip to Paso Robles, we heard a telling new piece of the story that lends it a measure of relatability and a delicious irony. When young Denner was getting close to old enough to leave home and strike out on his own, winery staff told us, he failed to demonstrate the seriousness his parents hoped to see in him. The gregarious Denner lacked direction. And so his parents warned their fun-loving but aimless son that unless he buckled down and got serious about his future, he would end up digging ditches for a living. Seen in the light of this rounded-out story, Denner, a self-described "dumb lucky guy," becomes a charming, self-deprecating underdog who had to struggle and grow to beat the odds, and the Ditch Digger name becomes a sly callback to his inauspicious beginnings.

Notice that this is the story of the birth of the winery and of the name of one of its most celebrated wines. It's the tale of a defining moment.

Why do winery staff routinely tell customers this origin story? One of them speculated that for visitors who may not be wine aficionados, the story provides an alternate way for them to connect with the winery and its wine. In a world awash in excellent wine, it promotes an indispensable relationship between the customer, this specific winery, and this uniquely named wine.

Farther south, in the western reaches of Santa Barbara County, Sanford Winery specializes in cool-climate pinot noir and chardonnay. Our daughter Hope Riley worked for Sanford as director of hospitality. In the tasting room, located in the middle of the vineyard in the idyllic Sta. Rita Hills, she worked with the winery staff to create wine-tasting experiences for their guests and wine club members. How did she do it? To a surprising degree, she did it by leading a team of storytellers who happen to pour wine.

When we told Hope the complete Ditch Digger story, she responded with professional appreciation. To her mind, a yarn about a rich guy who sells one successful business to build a successful winery doesn't represent a compelling or accessible story. But as soon as you add in the moment that Ron Denner's parents predicted he'd spend his life digging ditches, she saw the story becoming personal and emotional. She felt it connect.

"We've all been down on our luck and not sure what we wanted to do. And being a ditch digger or working at McDonald's for the rest of your life, there's this — " Here, Hope let out a small gasp of dread. "And now he owns a winery. And now he has a wine named Ditch Digger. And it's like, 'I, too, can do hard things.'"

Why does a story like this add so much value to the wine business? Because of the nature of the task. "My job," said Hope, "is to demystify wine and to make you feel like you got something out of this. And not just the wine. The story and the emotional connection." She added, "You have to help them understand why this is an $80 bottle of wine."

To do that, she used every available storytelling resource. Because the Sanford tasting room sits in the middle of the vineyard, she took advantage of the opportunity to apply the story maxim "show, don't tell."

"I love taking people out in the vineyard and putting dirt in their hands to have that tactile part of storytelling. We talk about the vines that struggle. What if you actually saw the vines that struggle? On an estate, you have the whole property as your backdrop. This is where the magic happens."

And after she'd taken them out among the vines and told them a compelling story of struggle, of a founder who drove up and down the California coast for years looking for the perfect location for his dream vineyard, of vines that defy rocky soil and years of drought and a shocking degree of what is called "vine mortality," and, as a last desperate act to propagate their ebbing life, produce a tiny yield of the best and most flavorful grape clusters, after she'd filled their hands with dirt and their glasses with the resulting pinot noir, something extraordinary happened. "You got to take that story home physically in a bottle."

Then something more happened, a phenomenon that extended beyond the telling of a tale followed by the sale of two or three bottles of wine. The visitors shared their own stories with the staff. One guest, a hospice doctor, described his own work to Hope, making explicit the connection between the suffering of the vines and the suffering of his patients and their families. As a result, said Hope, "You build an emotional connection. I'm getting something out of it, too, now, because I'm connecting on an emotional level through storytelling."

And which stories are the best stories to tell at a winery? Stories that make a difference, stories that narrate the crossing of the boundary between the before and the after, stories of the birth of a vineyard, the death of a vine, the realization of a dream. Defining moments.

The Businesses We Lead and Serve

It isn't just the winery business that can benefit from an understanding of the power of defining moments. Author and business consultant Annette Simmons, in her book *The Story Factor*,* highlights the importance of influence for anyone in business. Influence comes into play when businesspeople lead, market, sell, negotiate, collaborate, and innovate. Simmons urges businesspeople "to rediscover the oldest tool of influence in human history — telling a good story."

Story? Why not bombard colleagues and customers with information? Surely facts pack more persuasive power than stories.

---

* Annette Simmons, *The Story Factor: Inspiration, Influence, and Persuasion Through the Art of Storytelling*, revised ed., Basic Books, 2006.

"People don't want more information," Simmons insists. "They want faith — faith in you, your goals, your success, in the story you tell." Contrary to what we might think, she argues, stories are more powerful than facts. "Facts don't have the power to change someone's story. Their story is more powerful than your facts. As a person of influence, your goal is to introduce a new story that will let your facts in."

In particular, she advises businesspeople to tell stories that answer two primary questions: "Who are you?" and "Why are you here?" Stories of your personal defining moments, discoverable using the strategies described in Chapter 3, can address the "Who are you?" question head on. They may also demonstrate your most authentic, compelling, and disarming answer to the question "Why are you here?"

A third category of story Simmons recommends businesspeople maintain in their repertoire is what she calls the "vision story."

"You have to take the time to find a story of your vision in a way that connects — a story that people can *see*. The secret of a moving story is to tell it from a place of complete authenticity." A story of the vision toward which an enterprise is working does more than supply guidance. It provides a reason to persevere in the face of adversity. "A real vision story connects with people in a way that shrinks today's frustrations in light of the promise of tomorrow," Simmons writes. A story like that "gives our struggles meaning."

Where can you find a vision story?

- If you're the founder of the company, search your collection of personal defining moments for the story of the awakening of your dream for your company.

- If you're not the founder but you know that the vision of the enterprise drew you to work there, look back to the moment you discovered or committed yourself to the organization's cause.
- If you don't find a story in your personal history that relates to the company's vision, look to the history of the company itself. Businesses have origin stories. Over time, they grow and change, much like characters, and sometimes that change comes in convulsive moments of near death, of adversity, of reimagining, or of transformation. Applying the strategies described in Chapter 3 to your company, work to discover its defining moments and explore them for a vision story. In the same way that our friends can't really know us without knowing at least some of our defining moments, our employees, board members, executives, and customers can't really know and understand the company without knowing at least some of *its* defining moments. Which moments have defined the organization you lead? How was the company born? Who was there? What did they dream? Why did they work so hard to create this entity from nothing? Which insurmountable obstacles did they have to fight to overcome, and what did they sacrifice in order to establish this enterprise? The answers to these questions will likely lead you to some of your organization's defining moments.

Effective storytelling demands an essential, complementary skill: story-listening. Because successful business ventures thrive on collaboration — on the working relationships between colleagues, and on the relationships between companies and their customers — the stories of your colleagues and customers can provide you invaluable insight to help your organization grow, thrive, and even heal.

"Listening," wrote Edgar Rivera Colón, "is a primitive act of love in which a person gives himself to another's word, making himself accessible and vulnerable to that word."

To listen to the stories of your coworkers, whether board members, bosses, or subordinates, and to the stories of your customers requires patience, vulnerability, discipline, even courage. It requires you to care. More to the point, it requires you to put your care into action.

When you do stop talking and begin listening, *focus* your listening. Tune your ear to hear about experiences that possess a before-and-after quality. Take note of the stories you hear of experiences that display the characteristics of defining moments listed in Chapter 2. To understand the moments that have defined your CEO is to gain an enormous degree of understanding of your CEO. When you hear a subordinate talk about the moment that steered them into their field or that brought them to work at your company or that drove them out of their last job, you've gained insight that can help you increase their engagement and address the anxieties most likely to distract or derail them. And when you share stories of your own defining moments, you make yourself human, you strengthen your bonds with your collaborators, you foster the psychological safety essential to the thriving of creative teams,* and you help your partners understand how best to work with you.

Healers and Their Patients

Could an understanding of defining moments help doctors,

---

* For more on the role of psychological safety in the success of creative teams, see the chapter "Teams" in Charles Duhigg's *Smarter Faster Better: The Transformative Power of Real Productivity*, Random House, 2017.

nurses, and other medical professionals practice better medicine? The emerging field of narrative medicine, pioneered by Dr. Rita Charon and her colleagues at Columbia University starting in 2000, has begun to demonstrate the power of storytelling and story-listening to improve medical outcomes and even to reduce costs.

Charon and her coauthors write in the seminal text* of their new field, "Narrative medicine began as a rigorous intellectual and clinical discipline to fortify healthcare with the capacity to skillfully receive the accounts persons give of themselves — to recognize, absorb, interpret, and be moved to action by the stories of others."

The pioneers of narrative medicine write that they initiated their work melding story and healthcare because they'd come to believe that promoting narrative skills among medical professionals would allow them to sharpen and broaden their knowledge of their patients and deepen what they term "therapeutic partnerships" with those patients. The result, they believed, would be to improve healthcare in concrete and measurable ways.

When doctors and other healthcare providers gain skill in teasing out and then truly hearing the stories of their patients, they learn things they never can from lab tests and medical imaging alone. "Narrative competence," they write, "can widen the clinical gaze to include personal and social elements of patients' lives vital to the tasks of healing."

The practice of narrative medicine centers around what it calls three movements:

- **Attention:** a state of deep, attentive listening to the teller of the story.

---

* Rita Charon et al., *The Principles and Practice of Narrative Medicine*, Oxford University Press, 2017.

- **Representation:** a reflection on what is heard, usually written so it is visible to both the listener and the teller. It says, "This is what I think you told me," creating an opportunity for teller and listener to refine understanding.
- **Affiliation:** the natural result of the first two movements, a bond between provider and patient that allows them to journey together no matter where that journey may lead.

We propose that an understanding of the importance of defining moments, of the pivot points in a patient's life and health, and of the characteristics that distinguish those moments can enhance a healthcare provider's "narrative competence." Providers whose ears are tuned to hear and appreciate the significance of the before-and-after language that may emerge with a patient story will recognize that they are encountering a defining moment for the patient or the patient's health, one that may warrant closer scrutiny and that may lead to important therapeutic insights. Alternatively, providers armed with a knowledge of the characteristics of defining moments will ask questions shaped by that knowledge, increasing the likelihood that they will invite the patient to share stories that may aid in "the tasks of healing."

Kathy was so intrigued by the promise of narrative medicine and its blending of storytelling and healthcare — two disciplines that have overlapped to a profound degree in her own life — that she enrolled to study narrative medicine at Columbia. As a student in their certification of professional achievement program, she studied under Charon and the eclectic faculty drawn from both medicine and the humanities.

Since completing that program, she has led workshops rooted in the insights of narrative medicine for patients, caregivers, medical social workers, and others. These workshops help participants, most of whom are somehow involved in the emotionally arduous field of pediatric oncology, develop the ability to listen deeply to the stories of others so they can provide more effective care. They also help participants discover and articulate their own stories as a strategy of self-care. Hearing these stories deepens Kathy's understanding of participants and their experiences, strengthens her relationships with them, and both deepens and broadens her understanding of the patient and caregiver population.

Kathy finds that the stories that arise from participants in these workshops frequently center on moments of diagnosis with a life-threatening illness or moments when the participant gained a life-changing insight in the context of illness or healing. These experiences of discovery unearth defining moments.

Teachers and Learners

Every academic discipline has stories. The field of physics has many, featuring characters from Archimedes with his "Eureka!" moment to Isaac Newton and his retreat from Cambridge to his family farm in 1665 to shelter from the Great Plague, during which time he developed his groundbreaking theories that revolutionized math and physics. The broad field of history is built of stories that narrate the moments that matter, moments like 9/11 or the stock market crash of 1929 or the Normandy landings or the defeat of the Spanish Armada, that redefined some part of the world. Math, philosophy, chemistry, literature, government, psychology, economics, and even physical education all have stories. The most effective teachers, either by instinct or design, tell their students stories of these moments that made a difference. The stories, in turn, heighten student interest in class, promote their understanding of underlying concepts, and increase their retention of what they've learned by associating it with a meaningful and memorable narrative.

If every academic discipline has stories, so does every teacher. When Chris teaches screenwriting courses, he often tells students the story of the experience that awakened in him his dream of — and lifelong commitment to — writing movies. His story of seeing the film *Ordinary People*, related in Chapter 3, taught him two life-changing lessons, he tells students. Those lessons reshaped his life, took him from Kansas to Hollywood, where he spent many years struggling to learn how to write effective screenplays, and eventually led him into the classroom with the students he now addresses and hopes to equip with his own hard-won lessons. In other words, he tells them the story of a moment that radically redefined him. This story positions Chris as a character in his own story with whom students can identify as he struggles, learns meaningful lessons, and dreams. It's a story that includes his students, as it connects his journey with theirs. This relationship, this binding of his struggle to theirs, fosters an environment ripe for the creative risk-taking necessary for learning what he seeks to teach.

But it's not just academic disciplines and teachers who have stories. Students have them, too. Learning them is for teachers one of the great rewards of teaching. During his time directing the Act One Hollywood Writing Program, Chris learned an exercise from his colleague Barbara Nicolosi, at that time executive director of Act One, that helps aspiring screenwriters discover and articulate personal, meaningful stories. It's called the credo exercise (*credo* being Latin for "I believe"). Multiple credo exercises found online ask for a list of statements the writer believes to be true. Nicolosi's version goes beyond the mere listing of beliefs that a writer might have read or been told by others. It requires writers to tell the personal, true story that first proved to them the veracity of what they believe, connecting that belief to an autobiographical story. For example, a writer who asserts the belief that cheating in school only cheats the student out of an opportunity to learn might tell a story of the time they stole their geometry teacher's final exam answer key, got a perfect score on the exam and an A in the class, and preserved their GPA. But a year later, having bypassed the opportunity to master geometry, they floundered on the SAT, earned a disappointing score, and failed to get into the university of their dreams. The writer puts the story on paper and then reads the story to the class, allowing the story itself to demonstrate the truth of the writer's belief. The sharing of these stories results in writers receiving deep and moving insights into one another. They also gain enormous empathy for one another. Chris has since led writing students in this exercise countless times over many years. Students sometimes flounder, protesting that they're too young or haven't experienced anything remarkable enough to have taught them anything of note. Chris encourages them by saying that anyone who has survived middle school has a story. And eventually, everyone finds their truth and the story that taught it to them. They write it down and read it out loud to the class. In almost every case, students tell stories that grab and hold the attention of their classmates. These stories do more, however, than interest their listeners. They move those listeners — Chris included — with authentic emotion. And by definition, they add up to something meaningful. Often, they're so honest they feel dangerous. Sometimes, the storyteller loses, for a moment, the ability to speak. On rare occasions, they flee the classroom. Always, their classmates respond with empathy and support, rooting for the storyteller, feeling the emotions with them. Chris frequently struggles to compose himself so that he can continue teaching after he hears these stories. In the process, students and teacher get to know one another through the complementary acts of storytelling and story-listening as they take turns sharing deeply personal accounts of the moments that have defined their beliefs, and thereby defined them.

Novels and Netflix

We explored the value that an understanding of defining moments offers the people who make television, film, and books. What about the vastly larger group of people who watch and read their work? How can an understanding of defining moments help them?

Simply put, an awareness of defining moments helps viewers and readers understand why characters say what they say and do what they do. And it helps them understand what the story means. It helps them decode the story.

Jean Valjean, the protagonist of Victor Hugo's sprawling and much-loved 1862 novel *Les Misérables*, is shaped by one set of defining moments. His antagonist Javert is shaped by a starkly different set of moments. A reader trying to make sense of the 365 chapters of the novel, one of literary history's longest, will get lost in details if every long digression and every one of the novel's more than 650,000 words receives equal weight. But readers who understand the outsized significance of a handful of pivotal moments in a character's life will stand a much improved chance of latching onto the finite number of character-defining moments that the novel presents, allowing the reader to make sense of it.

For Valjean, the moment of his arrest for stealing a loaf of bread to feed his sister's children will anchor the list. The moment of his eventual release from prison will also get added. So will the moment Bishop Myriel mercifully lies to save Valjean from arrest and gives him two silver candlesticks, challenging him to sell the silver and use the money to make for himself an honest life.

When the reader learns that Javert, the police inspector fanatically devoted to the law who pursues Valjean across the decades, was born in prison, the child of convicts, that unexpected fact joins the list of Javert's defining moments. The moment Javert as a young man renounces his parents to become a prison guard, surely a pivotal event in the development of his character, assumes an equally prominent place on this list; this moment of Javert crossing over from identification with those who transgress the law to identification with those who enforce it demands the reader's close attention. Readers familiar with the nature of defining moments won't be able to ignore the before-and-after quality of this act. They will see it as the instant Javert reorients his life in a way that will define him up to the moment of his death. They will appreciate that this moment, out of the countless moments in this nearly 3,000-page novel, is in fact the key to understanding why Javert will one day, decades later, feel he has no choice but to leap to his death in the Seine.

Throw in Fantine and Cosette, and a reader could construct a concise and comprehensible synopsis of *Les Misérables* from little more than a list of its main characters' defining moments. And while that reader could expect many of the novel's details and expansive digressions to fall away in the process of the story's adaptation to the stage or screen, the reader can safely anticipate finding that an impressive number of each of the main characters' defining moments survive the translation. The essence of the story remains intact and is recognizable through that memorable constellation of defining moments.

An understanding of defining moments does more than help the audience understand the characters. It makes its meaning clear. When a reader tracks the trajectory of each character's defining moments over the course of *Les Misérables*, the novel's themes come into focus. A reader can look at the moments that define Valjean and Javert at their beginnings and at their ends. From the end of the novel, armed with a knowledge of each character's defining moments, a reader can retrace their journeys and ask what inner choices and outside forces directed those paths in order to discern what the story means.

Victor Hugo said as much in the early pages of his novel.

> The book which the reader has under his eye at this moment is, from one end to the other, as a whole and in detail, whatever may be its intermittences, exceptions and faults, the march from evil to good, from the unjust to the just, from night to day, from appetite to conscience, from rottenness to life, from hell to heaven, from nothingness to God. Point of departure: matter; point of arrival: the soul. The hydra at the beginning, the angel at the end.*

The Ones We Hold Dearest

If only the people we love followed such neat trajectories, traveling from hydra to angel in a compact series of transformative experiences and decisions. Is it possible they do? Or, at the very least, that understanding a finite number of their defining moments might open a window of comprehension that will make more loving relationships with them possible?

While a comprehensive guide to interpersonal communication, marriage, family therapy, and conflict management lies far beyond the scope of this book, we will offer at least a glimpse of the ways an awareness of defining moments can foster richer connections with the people in our inner circles.

Imagine two sisters living in Omaha, one four years older than the other. They've grown up together in the same tiny house with the same single father, a widower. Despite the age difference, they're close. They confide in one another, put on magic shows together, study together, miss their late mother together. The day

---

* Victor Hugo, *Les Misérables*, translated by Isabel F. Hapgood, Thomas Y. Crowell & Co., 1887.

the older one, Gretchen, a risk-taker who has sworn off college, turns seventeen, she flies off to spend the year in Switzerland as an exchange student. She hopes to spend the year snowboarding and then return to Colorado to work at a winter resort in the Rockies. The younger sister, Helga, thirteen, shy and bookish, starts middle school that same year. She dreams of a career in science or math.

Twelve months later, Gretchen returns to Omaha. She's now eighteen and bound for Stanford on a full scholarship to study economics. Helga is fourteen and bound for juvenile court on a charge of heroin possession with intent to distribute. On Gretchen's first night back home as the girls get ready to sleep in their old bedroom, Gretchen confronts Helga. How is it possible that she's dealing heroin? What the hell is wrong with her? Without a word, Helga grabs her blanket and pillow and walks from the room.

The once-close relationship between the sisters is severed. During their year apart, they've become different people. The critical question to ask, of course, is what happened?

If we're attuned to the power of defining moments, we will immediately suspect that each sister has experienced something that resulted in the profound changes we now observe. But by starting the conversation asking "What's wrong with you?" Gretchen deprives herself of the opportunity to learn about whatever has redefined Helga. Helga, in turn, has no opportunity to learn what has changed her once university-averse sister. Helga will also likely face whatever adversity she's experiencing without the support of her previously intimate friend and sister. When Gretchen flies off to Stanford in the fall, the young women will likely continue along their diverging paths, growing ever more distant from one another.

A strategy that's being used in medical and therapeutic environments turns this doomed approach on its head. A method known as trauma-informed care recognizes that a question such as "What's wrong with you?" undermines the sense of safety all humans crave, especially in the context of the surprisingly large fraction of people who have experienced some form of trauma or adversity. Instead, a trauma-informed approach asks, "What's happened to you?" Instead of judging, it inquires. It assumes, in fact, that experiences of trauma and adversity are so common that all people should be treated with the care and sensitivity represented by the shift in questions from "What's wrong with you?" to "What's happened to you?"

In a 2018 talk at TEDxUSF, Jamie Meyer, senior director of education at Metropolitan Ministries, a facility where one hundred homeless families reside, discussed her organization's experience with trauma-informed care and the difference it makes for residents and staff alike.

> Changing the question from "What's wrong with you?" to "What happened to you?" is a focus on the why behind the what . . . The what is the attitude or behavior we see in another, and the why is the reason behind it . . . Once we understand the why, we can begin to make real and lasting changes to the what . . . We spend time at the beginning with each individual, garnering their trust so they feel safe to share what's happened to them. They teach us, each and every one of them, their own personal why behind the what. We've learned about our own [experiences of trauma and adversity], and we connect on a level that reminds us we've all had things happen and we all want to be better . . . What might happen if we changed the question to "What happened to you?" and allowed the answer to teach us and push us to grow?*

Our purpose here is not to train readers to provide therapy to

* Jamie Meyer, TEDxUSF, May 31, 2018.

traumatized people. Our purpose is to borrow from the insights of trauma-informed care to make each of us better able to engage in healthy and healing relationships with the people we love. By assuming that a pivotal experience likely underlies otherwise inexplicable changes or behaviors in those closest to us, and by working to build trust, we create an environment in which we can invite our loved ones to share their stories with us. And when they do, we create the possibility that we will learn something new about them, something that generates compassion and empathy in us rather than judgment or rejection. When we hear the story, we see beyond the behavior to the person. We make space where we can join them and walk alongside them with understanding. And we increase the likelihood that we can share our own stories — sometimes stories of trauma or adversity, other times stories of healing or triumph — to enlarge the common ground we share with one another.

For Gretchen and her sister Helga, if either of them were to ask "What happened to you?" without judgment but with genuine humility and openness, they might share the stories of the events of the past year that have redefined them. If they did, the distance between them might narrow, and their paths might begin to converge.

What would happen in your own relationships if you did the same? How might an awareness of and a sensitivity to defining moments allow you to love the people dearest to you?

Afterword

"What quickens my pulse now is
the stretch ahead rather than the one behind,
and it is mainly for some clue to where I am going
that I search through where I have been,
for some hint as to who I am becoming
or failing to become
that I delve into what used to be."
— Frederick Buechner

We began this book with the promise that we would offer you the best of what we've come to understand about creating emotionally authentic characters who grow as they struggle. We introduced the concept of character-defining moments, and we introduced the characteristics those moments tend to share. We recalled the stories of some of television, cinema, and literature's most iconic characters and spotlit moments that made those characters who they became in our collective memories. We invited you to search out the moments that have defined you. We told stories of some of our own most personal, painful, healing, defining moments. At the outset, we said we hoped doing so would encourage and equip you to reveal yourself, both in the characters you create and in the life you lead. We began as strangers to one another. We hope that you've come to know us as we've revealed ourselves. We hope that you've come to know yourself as you've explored your own stories. And we hope that through your telling of those stories and the stories of the characters they inspire, we and millions of other viewers and readers will come to know you.

Appendix A

THE HERO QUESTIONS

What does the hero want? (external/superficial/requires no growth)

How does the hero need to grow and change? (internal/deep/transforming; what emotional agony is your hero — or the hero's "family" — suffering?)

What are we rooting for (in relation to this character)?

Why do we root for them?/How are they like us? (flaws/quirks/nobility/genius/drive/pain)

What terrible thing will happen if they don't get what they *want*?

What terrible thing will happen if they don't grow and change in the way they *need*?

What is the hero's initial plan to reach the goal?

What are the major obstacles that stand in the way of the hero reaching the goal?

Why does the hero's initial plan fail?

What events will happen to our hero that will force them to grow and change?

What is the hero's last, desperate plan, and why will it require their growth, and why will it succeed or fail?

THE HERO IN CONTEXT

What is the central relationship?

What is the core story?

Where is the story's star role?

Appendix B

THE EIGHT ESSENTIAL STORY POINTS

Act One: The Setup

1. **Opening** *(page 1*)*: The hook. Grab the reader with something visual, fresh, weird, or mysterious that asks questions whose answers we do not know. Something the audience has never seen before. Tells us important things about our hero and the status quo of their life. Should be consistent with genre. What makes this day special?
2. **Upsetting the Apple Cart** *(pages 10–15)*: An incident disrupts the status quo in the hero's world and sets their story in motion.
3. **End of Act One** *(pages 25–30)*: Something happens that cuts off any possible return to the status quo; our hero is shot out of a cannon or caught in a trap; they can't go back, they can only go forward; they are challenged at the point of their internal need for change.

Act Two: Rising Conflict

4. **Beginning of Act Two** *(page 30)*: Our hero makes a plan.
5. **Midpoint** *(pages 55–60)*: A major development spins the story in a new direction; the hero's plan is adjusted.
6. **End of Act Two** *(pages 80–85)*: A crisis; the hero's plan fails; all hope is lost.

---

* These page ranges are meant to serve as a guide for feature-length screenplays. Writers in other forms will need to adhere to different standard total page counts. Regardless of your form, you should grab your reader with the opening on the first page.

Act Three: Climax and Resolution

7. **Beginning of Act Three** *(pages 80–85)*: Our hero makes a new plan that requires them to grow and do something they've never done before at the most basic level of their deepest need for change. The new plan results from the hero, now a new person, relying on a new capability.
8. **End of Act Three** *(pages 105–115)*: A final showdown. The new plan succeeds (or fails), and our hero achieves their goal (or doesn't), often in an unexpected way that satisfies not the want but the need for growth and change.

About the Authors

Christopher Riley is a professional screenwriter who cowrote with his wife Kathy Riley the award-winning German language film *After the Truth*. The Rileys have written scripts for Disney's Touchstone Pictures, Paramount Pictures, Mandalay Television Pictures, Sean Connery's Fountainbridge Films, and Robert Cort Productions. Christopher produced the action-thriller *Red Line* and executive produced the web series *Bump+*. He began his career as a proofreader in the standard-setting script processing department at Warner Bros., a department he eventually rose to manage. He is the former director of the Act One Hollywood Writing Program, the author of the classic screenplay format guide *The Hollywood Standard*, an instructor of screenwriting at the undergraduate and graduate levels, a founding partner of the Story Masters Film Academy, and a longtime member of the Writers Guild of America West.

Kathy Riley cowrote the award-winning feature film *After the Truth*. In addition to her work as a writer for Touchstone Pictures, Paramount Pictures, Mandalay Television Pictures, Fountainbridge Films, and Robert Cort Productions, Kathy holds a master's degree in public health and is a certified health education specialist. She serves as vice president of family support for the Pediatric Brain Tumor Foundation and has worked extensively on behalf of families of children diagnosed with brain tumors. She also holds a certification of professional achievement in narrative medicine from Columbia University and is a longtime member of the Writers Guild of America West.

The Rileys have four adult children and live in Los Angeles. They can be reached by email at chrisariley@gmail.com.

THE HOLLYWOOD STANDARD, 3RD EDITION

THE COMPLETE AND AUTHORITATIVE GUIDE TO SCRIPT FORMAT AND STYLE

CHRISTOPHER RILEY

This is the definitive guide to professional script formats used in Hollywood, written by Hollywood's foremost authority, now updated to highlight formatting innovations by some of the industry's most creative screenwriters. With a foreword by Antwone Fisher, this is the guide used every day by professional screenwriters and top film schools.

This new edition of the classic formatting guide examines the future of formatting with a chapter on how Hollywood's most innovative screenwriters are pushing the boundaries of screenplay format. For the first time, it devotes a chapter to the quirks of formatting scripts for animation. Poor formatting is the mark of an amateur and in the ultra-competitive world of screenwriting, the guidance found in this book will guarantee that your script makes a winning first impression.

"The two crucial ingredients for an exceptional screenplay are a great idea and Christopher Riley's The Hollywood Standard. *Riley's guidance will ensure that your vision is communicated clearly and professionally to the people who will buy and make your film."*

–Sheryl Anderson, creator and executive producer (*Sweet Magnolias*, writer-producer, *Ties That Bind*, *Parker Lewis Can't Lose*, *Dave's World*, *Charmed*, *Flash Gordon*)

"One of the first books I tell new writers to buy. It is indispensable, practical, readable, and fun to use. Buy this book before you write another word!"

– Dean Batali, TV Writer/Producer (*That '70s Show*, *Buffy the Vampire Slayer*)

CHRISTOPHER RILEY is an American screenwriter whose first film, *After The Truth*, a multiple-award-winning courtroom thriller, sparked international controversy when it was released in Germany in 1999. Other credits include *25 To Life*, written for Touchstone Pictures, *The Other White House*, written for Sean Connery's Fountainbridge Films, *Aces*, written for Paramount Pictures and Emmy-winning producer Robert Cort, and an adaptation of the book *Actual Innocence*, for Mandalay Television Pictures and the Fox television network. He is a 14-year veteran of the Warner Bros. script department, and from 2005 through 2008, he served as director of the acclaimed Act One Writing Program in Hollywood. He executive produced the groundbreaking 2010 web series *Bump+* and produced the 2013 feature film, *Red Line*. He teaches screenwriting at John Paul the Great Catholic University and serves on the Pediatric Central Institutional Review Board for the National Cancer Institute..

$29.95 · 224 PAGES · ISBN: 9781615933228

FILM DIRECTING: SHOT BY SHOT

VISUALIZING FROM CONCEPT TO SCREEN

25TH ANNIVERSARY EDITION

STEVEN D. KATZ

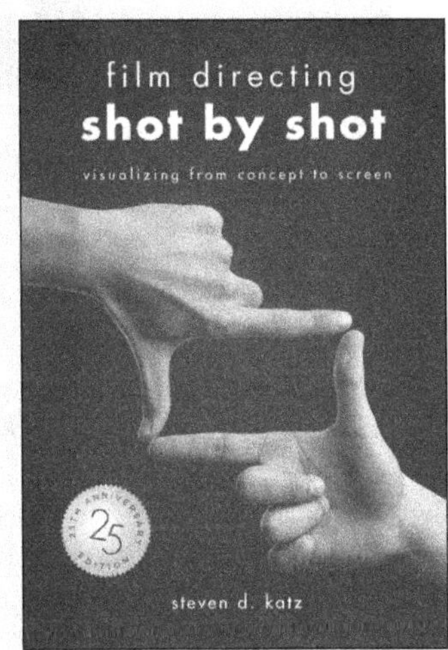

Shot by Shot is the world's go-to directing book, now newly updated for a special 25th Anniversary edition! The first edition sold over 250,000 copies, making it one of the bestselling books on film directing of all time. Aspiring directors, cinematographers, editors, and producers, many of whom are now working professionals, learned the craft of visual storytelling from *Shot by Shot*, the most complete source for preplanning the look of a movie.

The book contains over 800 photos and illustrations, and is by far the most comprehensive look at shot design in print, containing storyboards from movies such as *Citizen Kane*, *Blade Runner*, *Deadpool*, and *Moonrise Kingdom*. Also introduced is the concept of A, I, and L patterns as a way to simplify the hundreds of staging choices facing a director in every scene.

Shot by Shot uniquely blends story analysis with compositional strategies, citing examples then illustrated with the storyboards used for the actual films. Throughout the book, various visual approaches to short scenes are shown, exposing the directing processes of our most celebrated auteurs – including a meticulous, lavishly illustrated analysis of Steven Spielberg's scene design for *Empire of the Sun*.

Overall, the book has new storyboards and concept art, rewritten text for several chapters to address the needs of the YouTube generation of filmmakers, and an enhanced, expanded list of filmmaking resources.

- New introduction
- New storyboards: *Moonrise Kingdom*, *Deadpool*
- Six rewritten chapters detailing new trends and new digital production tools
- New section: Short Cuts
- Visual update: Dozens of illustrations are now shaded to maximize readability
- New bibliography
- New list of online resources

STEVEN D. KATZ is an award-winning writer, producer, and director. His work has appeared on *Saturday Night Live* and in many cable and theatrically released films, such as *Clear and Present Danger*, for which he completed the first full digital previsualization of a motion picture. He has taught workshops at the American Film Institute, Sundance Film Festival, Parsons School of Design, Danish Film Institute, School for Visual Arts (in New York), and Shanghai University, among many others.

$31.95 · 400 PAGES · ISBN 9781615932979

THE WRITER'S JOURNEY

MYTHIC STRUCTURE FOR WRITERS

25TH ANNIVERSARY EDITION

CHRISTOPHER VOGLER

Originally an influential memo Vogler wrote for Walt Disney Animation executives regarding *The Lion King*, The Writer's Journey details a twelve-stage, myth-inspired method that has galvanized Hollywood's treatment of cinematic storytelling. A format that once seldom deviated beyond a traditional three-act blueprint, Vogler's comprehensive theory of story structure and character development has met with universal acclaim, and is detailed herein using examples from myths, fairy tales, and classic movies. This book has changed the face of screenwriting worldwide over the last 25 years, and continues to do so.

"This book is like having the smartest person in the story meeting come home with you and whisper what to do in your ear as you write a screenplay. Insight for insight, step for step, Chris Vogler takes us through the process of connecting theme to story and making a script come alive."

—Lynda Obst, producer, How to Lose a Guy in 10 Days, Sleepless in Seattle, One Fine Day, Contact; Author, Hello, He Lied

"The Writer's Journey is an insightful and even inspirational guide to the craft of storytelling. An approach to structure that is fresh and contemporary, while respecting our roots in mythology."

—Charles Russell, writer, director, producer, Dreamscape, The Mask, Eraser

"The Writer's Journey should be on anyone's bookshelf who cares about the art of storytelling at the movies. Not just some theoretical tome filled with development clichés of the day, this book offers sound and practical advice on how to construct a story that works."

—David Friendly, producer, Little Miss Sunshine, Daylight, Courage Under Fire, Out to Sea, My Girl

CHRISTOPHER VOGLER made documentary films as an Air Force officer before studying film production at the University of Southern California, where he encountered the ideas of mythologist Joseph Campbell and observed how they influenced the story design of 1977's *Star Wars*. He worked as a story consultant in the development departments of 20th Century Fox, Walt Disney Pictures and Animation, and Paramount Pictures, and wrote an influential memo on Campbell's Hero's Journey concept that led to his involvement in Disney's *Aladdin*, *The Lion King*, and *Hercules*. After the publication of *The Writer's Journey*, he developed stories for many productions, including Disney's remake of *101 Dalmatians*, Fox's *Fight Club*, *Courage Under Fire*, *Volcano*, and *The Thin Red Line*.

$29.95 · 400 PAGES · ISBN: 9781615933150

© Michele Montez

MICHAEL WIESE PRODUCTIONS

In a dark time, a light bringer came along, leading the curious and the frustrated to clarity and empowerment. It took the well-guarded secrets out of the hands of the few and made them available to all. It spread a spirit of openness and creative freedom, and built a storehouse of knowledge dedicated to the betterment of the arts.

The essence of Michael Wiese Productions (MWP) is empowering people who have the burning desire to express themselves creatively. We help them realize their dreams by putting the tools in their hands. We demystify the sometimes secretive worlds of screenwriting, directing, acting, producing, film financing, and other media crafts.

By doing so, we hope to bring forth a realization of 'conscious media,' which we define as being positively charged, emphasizing hope, and affirming positive values like trust, cooperation, self-empowerment, freedom, and love. Grounded in the deep roots of myth, it aims to be healing both for those who make the art and those who encounter it. It hopes to be transformative for people, opening doors to new possibilities and pulling back veils to reveal hidden worlds.

MWP has built a storehouse of knowledge unequaled in the world, for no other publisher has so many titles on the media arts. Please visit www.mwp.com, where you will find many free resources and a 25% discount on our books. Sign up and become part of the wider creative community!

Michael Wiese, Co-Publisher
Geraldine Overton, Co-Publisher

MW

CPSIA information can be obtained
at www.ICGtesting.com
Printed in the USA
JSHW021915050222
22611JS00001B/1

9 781615 933372